INTRODUCING
ISSUES WITH
OPPOSING
VIEWPOINTS®

Body Image

Lauri S. Scherer, *Book Editor*

GREENHAVEN PRESS
A part of Gale, Cengage Learning

GALE
CENGAGE Learning·

Detroit • New York • San Francisco • New Haven, Conn • Waterville, Maine • London

Elizabeth Des Chenes, *Director, Publishing Solutions*

© 2013 Greenhaven Press, a part of Gale, Cengage Learning

Gale and Greenhaven Press are registered trademarks used herein under license.

For more information, contact:
Greenhaven Press
27500 Drake Rd.
Farmington Hills, MI 48331-3535
Or you can visit our Internet site at gale.cengage.com

For product information and technology assistance, contact us at

Gale Customer Support, 1-800-877-4253
For permission to use material from this text or product, submit all requests online at www.cengage.com/permissions

Further permissions questions can be e-mailed to permissionrequest@cengage.com

Articles in Greenhaven Press anthologies are often edited for length to meet page requirements. In addition, original titles of these works are changed to clearly present the main thesis and to explicitly indicate the author's opinion. Every effort is made to ensure that Greenhaven Press accurately reflects the original intent of the authors. Every effort has been made to trace the owners of copyrighted material.

Cover image ©Bine/Shutterstock.com.

LIBRARY OF CONGRESS CATALOGING-IN-PUBLICATION DATA

Body image / Lauri S. Scherer, book editor.
   p. cm. -- (Introducing issues with opposing viewpoints)
  Includes bibliographical references and index.
  ISBN 978-0-7377-6273-0 (hardcover)
  1. Body image. I. Scherer, Lauri S.
  BF697.5.B63B615 2012
  306.4'613--dc23
                                          2012024248

Printed in the United States of America
1 2 3 4 5 6 7 16 15 14 13 12

Contents

Chapter 3: How Can Body Image Be Improved?

Foreword

Indulging in a wide spectrum of ideas, beliefs, and perspectives is a critical cornerstone of democracy. After all, it is often debates over differences of opinion, such as whether to legalize abortion, how to treat prisoners, or when to enact the death penalty, that shape our society and drive it forward. Such diversity of thought is frequently regarded as the hallmark of a healthy and civilized culture. As the Reverend Clifford Schutjer of the First Congregational Church in Mansfield, Ohio, declared in a 2001 sermon, "Surrounding oneself with only like-minded people, restricting what we listen to or read only to what we find agreeable is irresponsible. Refusing to entertain doubts once we make up our minds is a subtle but deadly form of arrogance." With this advice in mind, Introducing Issues with Opposing Viewpoints books aim to open readers' minds to the critically divergent views that comprise our world's most important debates.

Introducing Issues with Opposing Viewpoints simplifies for students the enormous and often overwhelming mass of material now available via print and electronic media. Collected in every volume is an array of opinions that captures the essence of a particular controversy or topic. Introducing Issues with Opposing Viewpoints books embody the spirit of nineteenth-century journalist Charles A. Dana's axiom: "Fight for your opinions, but do not believe that they contain the whole truth, or the only truth." Absorbing such contrasting opinions teaches students to analyze the strength of an argument and compare it to its opposition. From this process readers can inform and strengthen their own opinions, or be exposed to new information that will change their minds. Introducing Issues with Opposing Viewpoints is a mosaic of different voices. The authors are statesmen, pundits, academics, journalists, corporations, and ordinary people who have felt compelled to share their experiences and ideas in a public forum. Their words have been collected from newspapers, journals, books, speeches, interviews, and the Internet, the fastest growing body of opinionated material in the world.

Introducing Issues with Opposing Viewpoints shares many of the well-known features of its critically acclaimed parent series, Opposing Viewpoints. The articles are presented in a pro/con format, allowing readers to absorb divergent perspectives side by side. Active reading questions preface each viewpoint, requiring the student to approach the material thoughtfully and carefully. Useful charts, graphs, and cartoons supplement each article. A thorough introduction provides readers with crucial background on an issue. An annotated bibliography points the reader toward articles, books, and websites that contain additional information on the topic. An appendix of organizations to contact contains a wide variety of charities, nonprofit organizations, political groups, and private enterprises that each hold a position on the issue at hand. Finally, a comprehensive index allows readers to locate content quickly and efficiently.

Introducing Issues with Opposing Viewpoints is also significantly different from Opposing Viewpoints. As the series title implies, its presentation will help introduce students to the concept of opposing viewpoints and learn to use this material to aid in critical writing and debate. The series' four-color, accessible format makes the books attractive and inviting to readers of all levels. In addition, each viewpoint has been carefully edited to maximize a reader's understanding of the content. Short but thorough viewpoints capture the essence of an argument. A substantial, thought-provoking essay question placed at the end of each viewpoint asks the student to further investigate the issues raised in the viewpoint, compare and contrast two authors' arguments, or consider how one might go about forming an opinion on the topic at hand. Each viewpoint contains sidebars that include at-a-glance information and handy statistics. A Facts About section located in the back of the book further supplies students with relevant facts and figures.

Following in the tradition of the Opposing Viewpoints series, Greenhaven Press continues to provide readers with invaluable exposure to the controversial issues that shape our world. As John Stuart Mill once wrote: "The only way in which a human being can make some approach to knowing the whole of a subject is by hearing what can be said about it by persons of every variety of opinion and studying all modes in which it can be looked at by every character of mind. No wise man ever acquired his wisdom in any mode but this." It is to this principle that Introducing Issues with Opposing Viewpoints books are dedicated.

Introduction

In December 2011 the trendy clothing company H&M made a startling admission about its holiday season catalogue. The slim, beautiful models displaying a new line of lingerie were not actually models. Rather, they were virtual women, digitally created mannequins that shared a uniform body type. H&M drew its clothing onto this perfect, fake body. Then it photographed real models' faces and superimposed their heads onto the bodies. The mannequins were then further altered so they mimicked realistic human features, such as freckles or dark or light skin tone.

H&M's photos highlighted the many ways in which technology increasingly informs body image. Some people, such as *New York Magazine* reporter Alex Reese, suggest that something is wrong with clothing that must be displayed on bodies that are completely fake. "If even a model's real-life frame can't be trusted to show off H&M's clothing, it seems odd to tweak the body instead of the garment in question,"[1] he wrote. Noting that the skin of one of the model-mannequin hybrids had been tinted brown, editors at the feminist website Jezebel joked, "[At least] you can't say that the fictional, Photoshopped, mismatched-head future of catalog modeling isn't racially diverse." Fearing an era in which fake photos set the standard for what bodies and clothing should look like, the Jezebel editors added, "In the future, even models' faces won't be considered perfect enough for online fast fashion, and we'll buy all of our clothing from cyborgs."[2]

H&M's virtual models are no rarity. Images are so often retouched and altered that it is the minority of advertisements that have not gone under the digital knife. A 2010 investigation by the British tabloid the *Sun*, for example, found that 28 percent of cosmetics ads surveyed included fine print disclosing that pictures had been digitally enhanced, while 44 percent of ads looked enhanced but did not include any acknowledgment of enhancement. Just 28 percent of the ads were suspected of showing the cosmetic and model accurately.

For Seth and Eva Matlins, of the group Off Our Chests, this percentage is too low, and in an attempt to reverse this trend the Matlins have proposed that Congress pass the Media and Public Health Act.

This "truth in advertising" proposal would require companies to disclose whether images in their advertisements have been digitally altered. Citing an "epidemic crisis of confidence" for girls and women, the Matlins worry that unrealistic images skew girls' and women's images of themselves and distort their understanding of what they can realistically look like. "Too many look at these images and think they should look LIKE these images. And they can't . . . because they're not real," explain the Matlins. "So let's call a duck a duck and a modified picture a modified picture. All we're asking is that if you do it—you tell us you did."[3]

Although thousands of people have signed a petition in support of the Media and Public Health Act, others are unconvinced it is an appropriate response to digitally altered photographs. They challenge the premise of the act, saying not only that it is not the government's job to promote self-esteem but that it is unnecessary to require advertisers to disclose their use of this increasingly common technique. As journalist, blogger, and writer Tracee Sioux has put it, "No one under 80 doesn't know that advertising is Photoshopped. In fact, tweens and teenagers are better at using Photoshop than Photoshop artists employed by magazines. Why do people presume that kids are idiots who don't understand computers? They come out of the womb Internet savvy."[4] For Sioux and others, a better approach to boosting self-esteem and positive body image is to promote it in classrooms, clubs, and around family dinner tables.

Even though it may be common knowledge that ads and other images are digitally enhanced, coming face-to-face with that reality has been shown to boost the self-esteem of young girls. A 2010 study published in the *British Journal of Health Psychology* found that girls who watched a short video showing the extent to which models are enhanced are less prone to feel bad when they see pictures of them. More than 125 students aged ten to thirteen were shown a wildly popular video produced by the Dove Campaign for Real Beauty, in which a plain, somewhat greasy looking woman is transformed into a stunning model. "Evolution," which as of early 2012 had been viewed by more than 14 million people, shows this woman tended to by an entire team of make-up and hair artists. After she is styled, her image is digitally edited. Her face is separated from her neck, giving her a beautiful, but physically impossible, elongated look. Her eyes are digitally widened, and parts of her shoulders are erased.

Even for those aware of digital enhancement, the video offers a fascinating inside perspective on the extent to which an image can be altered. Researchers found that exposing girls to these details protected their self-esteem. They reported that the girls who saw the video and were next shown images of models reported no change in self-esteem. Meanwhile, girls who did not view "Evolution" suffered a drop in "body esteem" and "body satisfaction" upon looking at photos of models.

Whether self-esteem can or should be legislated, and the extent to which body image suffers from digitally altered images, are among the many questions and issues considered in *Introducing Issues with Opposing Viewpoints: Body Image*. The selections included in this volume expose readers to the basic debates surrounding body image and encourage them to develop their own opinions on this highly personal and engaging topic.

Notes

1. Alex Reese. "H&M's New Lingerie Models Are Computer-Generated." *New York Magazine*, December 5, 2011. http://ny mag.com/daily/fashion/2011/12/hms-new-lingerie-models-are -computer-generated.html.
2. "H&M Puts Real Model Heads on Fake Bodies." Jezebel.com. December 5, 2011. http://jezebel.com/5865114/hm-puts-real -model-heads-on-fake-bodies.
3. Quoted in "Women's Rights Petition: Protect Our Girls and Pass the Media and Public Health Act." Change.org, 2012. www .change.org/petitions/protect-our-girls-and-pass-the-media-and -public-health-act.
4. Tracee Sioux. "The Self-Esteem Act Is a Stupid Waste of Time." The Girl Revolution, October 18, 2011. http://thegirlrevolution .com/the-self-esteem-act-is-a-stupid-waste-of-time/.

Chapter 1

Who Is Affected by Body Image Problems?

Although all kinds of people are susceptible to concerns about body image, young women are most commonly affected.

Negative Body Image Is a Critical Problem for Women

Amy Swanson

"Body image problems are serious and deadly."

In the following viewpoint Amy Swanson argues that negative body image is a serious problem for women. She explains that women are forced to live up to unreasonable, unfair, and unhealthy beauty standards. When they cannot, they feel bad about themselves and become at risk for eating disorders like anorexia (in which a person deprives herself of food) or bulimia (in which a person vomits after eating). Eating disorders cause severe health problems and can even kill. For this reason, Swanson contends that body image problems are serious and must be dealt with.

Swanson is a special projects editor for the Nebraska newspaper the *McCook Daily Gazette.*

Amy Swanson, "Body Image Is Serious Stuff," *McCook Daily Gazette,* May 9, 2008.

AS YOU READ, CONSIDER THE FOLLOWING QUESTIONS:
1. What are the thoughts of a woman with a body image problem, according to the author?
2. What health problems does bulimia nervosa cause, according to Swanson?
3. What does the author say fades over time?

A young woman looks at herself in the mirror and despises what she sees. Deluded by the commercials that blare from her television screen, she is convinced that she is fat and ugly. No person, fact, or maxim will convince her otherwise. She is sure that she is hopelessly overweight and will be for the rest of her life. She is sure that no man will ever find her beautiful. She is forever dieting. Another young woman, with the same convictions, takes it a step farther. She starves herself. Even though she is beautifully slim, she is convinced that she is fat. Another young woman binges and purges. Another simply can't stop eating, even though she longs to lose weight. All of these young women have one thing in common: a body image problem.

Ridiculous Social Standards

Body image has been a huge issue for the Western world since the Roman Era, but never was it so pronounced until the advent of the Victorian Era. Victorian women had ridiculous stipulations of beauty placed on them—they were expected to be "pleasingly plump" everywhere but their waist, where they were expected to be ridiculously slim. These women disfigured their bodies with corsets, which broke their ribs and displaced and damaged digestive organs.

Today, corsets have gone out of fashion, but ridiculous societal standards have taken their place. A woman with a boyish, skeletal figure is held up as more attractive than a "pleasingly plump" one. In fact, the "pleasingly plump" woman will no doubt be held up as an example of how bad the obesity crisis in America is. The result? Hundreds of women are completely dissatisfied with their bodies, even when they are within a reasonable weight. I know several women who have a beautiful, slim body but are still convinced that they are fat.

Victorian women were expected to be "pleasingly plump" yet have very small waists, which led them to wear corsets that often broke ribs and damaged internal organs.

Poor Body Image a Serious Problem

So what's wrong with a little body image problem? Aren't most people discontent with some aspect of their body? The answer is yes, but a body image problem implies a far more dangerous thing than just discontentment. It is discontentment leading to disorder. Body image problems often lead to eating disorders, which in addition to mental anguish, cause a whole host of other health problems.

By far, the worst part of an eating disorder is the mental anguish that it causes. Imagine that you are one of the women described above. Your whole life long, nothing ever fit you right the first time you tried on a piece of clothing. Your whole life long, you looked at yourself in the mirror and hated what you saw. Your whole life long, the media and fashion market subtly put you down and convinced you that you weren't slim enough. After a while, it all builds up. Hatred of the body easily leads to hatred of the self. An eating disorder leads to depression. Depression leads to suicide. Body image problems are a serious thing indeed.

When Poor Body Image Leads to Death

And what can be done? The concept of equating beauty with slimness permeates our society. The hype about the obesity crisis can only lead to another crisis—an eating disorder crisis, which is one far more deadly and dangerous. Diabetes and hypertension can kill eventually, but an eating disorder can kill within months. People with anorexia nervosa can die of starvation; people with bulimia nervosa can bleed to death from esophagus erosion. Even worse, the depression that usually accompanies an eating disorder can cause suicidal thoughts and tendencies.

Is America racing toward a nation of depressed, disorder-ridden people by emphasizing skinniness in the media?

In this superficial American society, it is easy to forget where real beauty comes from. I am reminded of a line from the Jim Carrey

Women Have Negative Thoughts About Their Bodies

A 2011 survey by *Glamour* magazine found that 97 percent of women think at least one bad thought about their body every day. Researchers found that on average, women have thirteen negative body thoughts daily, or nearly one for every hour they are awake.

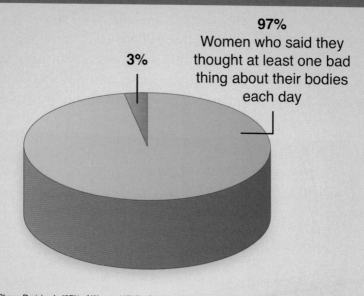

3%

97%
Women who said they thought at least one bad thing about their bodies each day

Taken from: Shaun Dreisback. "97% of Women Will Be Cruel to Their Bodies Today." *Glamour*, February 2011. www.glamour.com/health-fitness/2011/02/shocking-body-image-news-97-percent-of-women-will-be-cruel-to -their-bodies-today?currentPage=1.

movie "Liar Liar." In response to the phrase "Real beauty is on the inside," Carrey's character comments that "That's just what ugly people say to make themselves feel better." This type of mentality is hurtful and destructive, and not at all funny as it is made out to be. It's an old adage, but real beauty is on the inside. External beauty fades over time, but the intellect and the personality grow more rich and beautiful over time. This body that we live in is simply a house. Do we love the houses or the people inside of them? It is what is inside that counts. The saying is very old and perhaps a little trite, but it still rings true. America seems to have forgotten this entirely, and it is affecting people throughout the nation.

Fighting the Problem

Fortunately, there are organizations that are fighting against the unrealistic standards of American beauty. Dove recently sponsored "The Campaign for Real Beauty" and there are hundreds of other organizations that are working to help women of all ages feel good in the skin they're in. And fortunately, there is help for anyone who is afflicted by an eating disorder. Counseling and medical attention are the best solution for an eating disorder. Many communities have a body image support group of some kind. Why not start one in your own community? No matter how small your town, I'm sure that you will find that at least 10 people suffer from a body image problem of some kind.

The bottom line: Eating disorders and body image problems are serious and deadly. If anyone you know suffers from this terrible affliction, encourage them to seek medical attention immediately.

EVALUATING THE AUTHOR'S ARGUMENTS:

Amy Swanson uses examples, history, and reasoning to make her argument that body image is a serious problem. She does not, however, use any facts or statistics to support her case. Using your school library or the Internet, find at least two facts or statistics that could be used to support her argument. These could be the results of an opinion poll or a demographic study. Make sure the source from which the fact or statistic comes is authoritative and credible.

Girls Struggle with Negative Body Image

Kate Harding

"An overwhelming desire to be as thin as possible is gripping children ever younger and ever more tightly."

In the following viewpoint Kate Harding argues that a majority of girls struggle with negative body image. Worse, she explains, more girls struggle with images of themselves each year, and they continue to do so when they grow into women. Girls diet at increasingly young ages, and most equate thinness with public and social approval. Harding suggests that the nation's fixation with childhood obesity is partly to blame. She asserts that obesity-prevention programs cause girls to obsess about their bodies, and she faults them for promoting thinness rather than health. She concludes it is immoral to burden young girls with anything but a desire to be healthy and feel good about themselves.

Harding is a writer for the feminist website Jezebel.com.

AS YOU READ, CONSIDER THE FOLLOWING QUESTIONS:

1. Who is Jeffrey Zaslow? How does he factor into the author's argument?
2. What percentage of fourth-grade girls does Harding say believe one must be thin to be popular?
3. Who is Claire Mysko and how does she factor into Harding's argument?

In 1986, 80% of fourth-grade girls were dieting. [*Wall Street Journal*] reporter Jeffrey Zaslow interviewed 100 of them back then, and recently followed up with a few, asking if they think things are getting better for girls. The verdict: It's even worse.

Some Girls Never Escape

Furthermore, writes Zaslow, "Those girls I interviewed are 32 and 33 years old now, and when I got back in touch with some of them [in September 2009], they said that they and their peers have never escaped society's obsession with body image. While none of them descended into eating disorders, some told stories of damaging diets and serious self-esteem issues regarding their weight." Gee, I love a happy ending!

In other cheery news, Zaslow's interviewees were right: It's gotten worse. These days, eating disorders are on the rise, girls as young as five are preoccupied with body image, and "Between 2000 and 2006, the percentage of girls who believe that they must be thin to be popular rose to 60% from 48%."

Girls' Body Image Has Worsened

For about as long as I've been literate, journalists have been wringing their hands about little girls' body image problems in articles like the ones Zaslow wrote then and now. And yet, it hasn't gotten better. And people still act all shocked when they hear the latest statistics, as if it was OK when only around half of little girls believed thinness was a requirement for being popular—i.e., being *liked*—but 60%, whoa! That's just terrible! The question is, what are we going to do before another 20 years go by, and it's up to 75 or 80%, with 100% of fourth-grade girls dieting and new studies showing that female infants are worried their diapers make their butts look fat?

> ## FAST FACT
>
> A 2011 poll of nearly a thousand *Girl's Life* readers found that about 80 percent found fault with their own bodies, and 80 percent have dieted to lose weight.

For those of you who were horrified by my suggestion that we should focus on encouraging healthy behavior for its own sake and quit freaking out about childhood obesity, this is one reason why I

I'm s00 hungry!

"I'm s00 hungry!" cartoon by Wilbur Dawbarn, www.CartoonStock.com. Copyright © by Wilbur Dawbarn. Reproduction rights obtainable from www.CartoonStock.com.

suggest that, and suggest it passionately. Zaslow notes that Claire Mysko, former director of the American Anorexia Bulimia Association (and, disclosure, an acquaintance of mine), "worries that childhood obesity-prevention efforts can make girls obsessive about weight." He also writes that a study published earlier this year [2009] in the *Journal of Psychosocial Nursing* found preoccupation with body image "can be exacerbated by our culture's increased awareness of obesity,

Girls are especially concerned about their weight because most of them equate thinness with social and public approval.

which leaves many non-overweight kids stressed about their bodies." (FYI, it also leaves overweight kids stressed about their bodies, but I guess we're supposed to think that's OK; obviously, there's ample evidence to suggest that feeling ugly, disgusting, frustrated, left out and ashamed leads directly to healthy weight loss. Just look around you.)

We Have *Lost Our Minds* About Fat

A lot of things have changed since 1986—including, as Mysko points out, far more extreme retouching of images of the women who represent our culture's beauty standard—but one of the most obvious should be that we have *lost our minds* about fat. Whether or not obesity is as dramatic a public health crisis as we've been led to believe, the overwhelming message has been that *individuals* are responsible for solving it. Which means every day, the news brings dozens of new exhortations to lose weight in order not only to prevent your own early demise, but to lift the burden on our health care system and restore America's glory. For all but the thinnest of us, weight loss is cast not merely as a potential step toward better personal health but a moral obligation to society, to your children, to your partner, and to people who don't want to sit next to a fatty on the subway.

And we're supposed to be surprised that an overwhelming desire to be as thin as possible is gripping children ever younger and ever more tightly? Forgive me if I'm not.

EVALUATING THE AUTHOR'S ARGUMENTS:

Kate Harding blames childhood obesity-prevention efforts for promoting negative body image among increasingly young girls. Do you agree? Do you think obesity-prevention efforts protect girls' health, or do they promote a dangerous preoccupation with body image? Explain your reasoning.

Men with Distorted Body Images

Lisa Liddane

"A growing number of men . . . battle with what is still largely perceived as a woman's mental health condition."

Increasing numbers of boys and men struggle with negative body image, reports Lisa Liddane in the following viewpoint. While eating disorders are commonly viewed as afflicting girls and women, Liddane says that millions of men have eating disorders that stem from poor body image and a pressure to look strong, chiseled, and thin. She reports all different kinds of men feel these pressures—gay and straight men, men who are athletic, men who are obese, and men who are insecure. Although genetics may play a role, Liddane says that media geared toward males—such as magazines and toys—promote a lean and muscular physique that is often unattainable and unrealistic. She concludes that men need help combating poor body image just as much as women.

Liddane is a reporter for McClatchy Tribune Newspapers, a news service that services a variety of newspapers, including the *Chicago Tribune.*

AS YOU READ, CONSIDER THE FOLLOWING QUESTIONS:
1. About how many American men have eating disorders, as reported by Liddane?
2. What is body dysmorphia disorder, and how does Liddane say it specifically affects men?
3. What would GI Joe Extreme's measurements be if he were a life-size person, according to Liddane?

The secret signs of bulimia and anorexia are familiar.

Looking in the mirror and always seeing an unfit, unattractive, fat person—even when the real reflection isn't. Purging in the restroom after eating dinner with friends. Starving oneself by eating only one meal a day. Thinking constantly about one's body.

But the person in the mirror is not familiar.

It's a man.

His name is Dick. The 32-year-old sales associate from Anaheim asked that his last name not be used. None of his family members, friends and co-workers knows that he has been struggling for more than a decade with a distorted body image.

Dick is among a growing number of men—about 1 million in the United States, by most estimates—who battle with what is still largely perceived as a woman's mental health condition. The numbers of men with eating disorders may be greater—from 3 million to 5 million, said Roberto Olivardia, clinical psychologist at McLean Hospital in Belmont, Mass. Olivardia is co-author of *The Adonis Complex: The Secret Crisis of Male Body Obsession* (Free Press, $25).

Male eating disorders are underdiagnosed because society lacks awareness of them and men are less likely to admit they have this medical problem and seek help, Olivardia said.

That's changing slowly, he said.

Knowing who might be at risk may help prevent eating disorders from developing, say body-image researchers. Understanding the nature of male body obsession and eating disorders may help men recognize that they have these conditions and seek treatment.

Doctors and psychologists do not know the exact causes of distorted body images and eating disorders in men because research in these areas is in the infancy stages.

But more studies on men and boys are emerging in medical publications such as the *International Journal of Eating Disorders Research*.

One in six men may have anorexia and bulimia, according to a 1999 study in *Psychiatric Annals*, by Dr. Arnold E. Andersen, an eating-disorder researcher at University of Iowa.

Andersen classifies at-risk men into four groups:

- Men in sports and athletic activities who need to control weight for performance. This is the most prevalent group.
- Men who were overweight or obese and had negative, sometimes traumatic experiences related to their weight.
- Men whose fathers had ill health, possibly weight-related, or may have died because of it.
- Men who want to improve their body image. This includes gay and straight men.

Researchers have coined a term for one type of male body obsession: body dysmorphia disorder (BDD). An example of BDD is muscle dysmorphia, sometimes called "reverse anorexia" or "biggerexia." This disorder occurs when normal-size or big, muscular men think of themselves as thin and scrawny. Some men with muscle dysmorphia may be workout-aholics, or users of steroids or muscle-enhancing supplements.

Researchers also know that the effects of eating disorders on men are similar to those on women: weakened, fragile bones, elevated risk for heart attacks because of electrolyte imbalance, tooth decay, gastrointestinal problems and damage to the esophagus.

One theory in research that is gaining ground is the genetic link. Scientists suspect that the predisposition to an eating disorder may run in some families and in both sexes.

But genes aren't the only factors to blame. In the past decade, magazines such as *Men's Health* have perpetuated the myth that the look of male health is lean, low in fat, with Michelangelo-chiseled musculature, said Lynne Luciano, author of *Looking Good: Male Body Image in America*. Luciano is assistant professor of history at University of California, Dominguez Hills.

Lean and muscular physiques also are glorified in sports, TV, movies, music videos, advertising. They're even in toys. If GI Joe Extreme—the enhanced version—had been life-size, Luciano said, he would have a 32-inch waist, 44-inch chest and impossible 32-inch biceps.

The danger of these images, Olivardia said, is they create a blueprint for the masculine man that is difficult for most men to follow without resorting to drastic, unhealthy measures, such as taking steroids, muscle-enhancing supplements, using laxatives, working out obsessively, becoming anorexic and/or bulimic.

Distorted body images and eating disorders are often the manifestation of other problems, Olivardia said. Low self-esteem in childhood, adolescence and adulthood, psychological, emotional and mental issues can drive men to focus on their body or specific parts such as the midsection and see themselves as incredibly physically flawed.

Some people with a history of obsessive behaviors carry these over into their eating habits as a form of control, said Sarah Steinmeyer,

Athletic men are the most common group of males to have anorexia or bulimia.

psychologist at South Coast Medical Center Eating Disorders Program in Laguna Beach.

"Eating disorders are rarely about food," she said. "Food is a metaphor for other aspects of life. A man with an eating disorder and body obsession sometimes thinks he can control food, but food actually controls him."

South County resident Terry Murphy, 53, loathes what he sees when he looks in the mirror—an out-of-shape, overweight man. At 6 feet and 210 pounds, the management consultant said he feels he has no control over his body and is depressed about it.

"I can't get it out of [my] mind," Murphy said. "I think about it at least a dozen times a day."

> ## FAST FACT
>
> The Campaign for a Commercial Free Childhood reports that when presented with images of men and asked to choose which image represented a physical ideal, more than half of boys aged eleven to seventeen selected an image that was only possible to achieve by using steroids.

Murphy, who said he never had weight issues before, put on pounds over the years when a heart condition prevented him from maintaining six-day-a-week, one-and-a-half-hour intense workouts. Murphy continues to exercise most days of the week, but has reduced the intensity for the sake of his heart.

So he diets. His breakfast: a regular-size beef patty and cottage cheese. Lunch consists of a protein drink and a banana or an apple. Dinner is a low-calorie salad with chicken, half a glass of milk and the occasional small cookie.

Dick, like Murphy, feels frustrated and alone.

"Ever since I can remember, my physical appearance has been a way of gauging my self worth," Dick said.

Dick's weight for most of his teens was normal, but when he turned 19, he gained weight. At 5 feet, 6 inches, he weighed 195 pounds. After a routine physical exam, the doctor told him he was obese.

To lose weight, Dick did several things. He starved himself in private. And when he ate out with friends, he consumed a normal amount of food. But shortly after, he would excuse himself from the

The National Association of Anorexia Nervosa and Associated Disorders (ANAD) reports that boys and men suffer from negative body image and disordered eating, with men comprising between one and two out of every ten people who suffer from anorexia or bulimia. Whereas females feel pressure to be thin, males feel pressure to be chiseled, lean, and muscular.

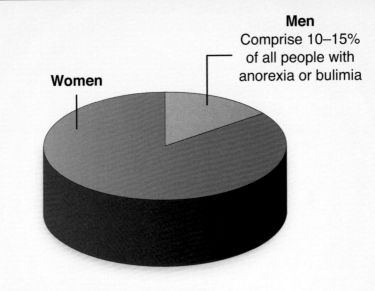

Women

Men
Comprise 10–15% of all people with anorexia or bulimia

Taken from: The National Association of Anorexia Nervosa and Associated Disorders, 2011.

table, go to the public restroom and make himself vomit. "The sooner I could purge, the easier it would be get the food out," he said.

He exercised relentlessly most days of the week, sometimes more than once a day.

Within a year, he lost 40 pounds.

Dick knew what he was doing was not healthy. But he kept it a secret. He was ashamed to talk about it with anyone. "It's a girl's disease," he said.

In 1989, a roommate caught him purging. At the friend's urging, he found a doctor who treated eating disorders. "The doctor tried to scare me with statistics and stories of girls who had died because of ruptures to their esophagus. I went three times for regular counseling. And then, I stopped. I thought I could do this on my own."

And he stopped bulimic behavior for six years. His weight stabilized at about 155 pounds. But his esophagus had been damaged from years of regurgitating food.

After a painful divorce several years ago, Dick returned to some unhealthy behaviors.

He takes nothing but coffee throughout the day. His only meal is at night.

"I don't know that I'm over it," he said.

Dick has tried to look for local men's support groups—to no avail. He does not feel comfortable attending women's anorexia and bulimia support groups. "That happens fairly often to men who are trying to get help," Steinmeyer said. "And that's terrible because the lack of support groups for men only perpetuates the myth that this is only a woman's disease."

When men seek help, they are in the advanced stages of their eating disorders because it takes them a long time to recognize and admit that they have a serious health problem and to develop the courage to communicate their need for help, said Jane Supino, executive director for the Center for the Study of Anorexia and Bulimia in New York.

Treatments for men are the same as women's—they are tailored to the individual. They vary from outpatient visits to hospital confinement for days, weeks or months. They may include intense nutritional intervention, such as intravenous feeding, if needed. Olivardia said treatment programs that target the problems from many angles with a team approach—involving the primary doctor, a psychologist or psychiatrist, a nutritionist and support groups—are likely to have best results.

EVALUATING THE AUTHOR'S ARGUMENTS:

Lisa Liddane quotes from several sources to support the points she makes in her essay. Make a list of everyone she quotes, including their credentials and the nature of their comments. Then, analyze her sources—are they credible? Are they well qualified to speak on this subject? What specific points do they support?

Body Image Problems Are Cross-Cultural

Montecatini Eating Disorder Treatment Center

"Body image problems are rapidly becoming more serious and widespread among women of all ethnic groups."

The Montecatini Eating Disorder Treatment Center is a rehab center located in San Diego, California. In the following viewpoint the author argues that body image problems affect women of all cultures. In the past, eating disorders and other body image problems primarily affected white women, but in recent years, says the author, socioeconomic and cultural factors, along with a barrage of influential media, have encouraged the development of poor body image and eating disorders in African American women, Hispanic women, and Asian American women. Some of these women face pressure to look white; others are predisposed to a larger body type, which makes them pine after an unattainable thinness. The center concludes that women of all cultures and ethnicities are at risk for having poor body image and the problems that come along with it.

AS YOU READ, CONSIDER THE FOLLOWING QUESTIONS:
1. What does the author say has changed about the way African American women view their bodies?
2. What physical pressures do Hispanic women face, according to the Montecatini Center?
3. What surgeries do Asian American women increasingly undergo, according to the author?

In a disturbing trend, research over the last two decades shows that body image problems are rapidly becoming more serious and widespread among women of all ethnic groups. As recently as the mid-'90s, all the studies revealed that Caucasian women were much more susceptible to negative body image issues and eating disorders than African-American, Asian-American or Hispanic women. But in the last few years, things have begun to level out among all U.S. groups.

All Ethnicities Are at Risk

In the past, women from Asian-American, African-American and Hispanic descent were given a safety net from body image problems by the unique cultural norms of their respective groups. For example, African-American cultural norms made it more likely for these women to reject external beauty standards and to emphasize inner beauty and strength while identifying with a heritage that assigns beauty to shapely bodies.

This helped create a relatively high self-worth among fuller-figured black women. But all of this has begun to change.

While these cultural safety nets haven't entirely disappeared, the power of the 21st Century media environment has changed things. The fact is, across all ethnicities, the average person spends more time in front of the television and the Internet than ever before. Our lives are media saturated, and this inevitably shapes our concept of beauty.

When faced with a steady bombardment of television and movie stars—most of whom are Caucasian—who uphold seemingly impossible standards of beauty and body shape, it's easy for the ordinary

Black Women and Eating Disorders

A study published in the *Archives of Family Medicine* found black women were significantly more likely to engage in fasting, laxative abuse, and diuretic abuse. Diuretics, which increase the discharge of urine, are sometimes abused for weight loss. Other studies have confirmed that negative body image and eating disorders are an increasing problem for women of color.

Symptoms During Preceding Three Months	Black Women %	White Women %
Fasting	4.1	2.7
Self-induced vomiting	1.2	0.9
Laxative abuse	2.1	0.8
Diuretic abuse	2.9	1.7

Taken from: Ruth H. Striedel-Moore et. al. "Recurrent Binge Eating in Black American Women." *Archives of Family Medicine*, Vol. 9., No. 1, January 2000.

woman to feel as though she doesn't measure up. And as the national and global media grow in everyday importance, local cultures fall by the wayside. This leads to a homogenized, one-size-fits-all standard of beauty that fewer and fewer people can live up to.

In addition to the Caucasian-centric media environment, there's also the sad fact that the average American's health is simply not as good as it used to be. This applies equally to women and men. We exercise less than we used to, we eat larger meals and more processed foods, and we work longer hours.

All of these things contribute to the well-documented obesity epidemic, which comes with other serious issues, including diabetes, cardiovascular disease, hypertension, depression, poor sleep and eating disorders. While the rise in obesity spans all ethnicities, it particularly affects the poorer segments of society, which in the U.S. are disproportionately black and Hispanic.

Women of All Colors Struggle

African-American women: Historically, African-American women have had to define their own standards of beauty, which helped give them relatively healthy self-images for a long time. Today, within the community, African-Americans are still less judgmental of one another's body types than other groups tend to be. However, increasing obesity combined with increasing media saturation is leading to a stark rise in eating disorders among African-American teenagers and young women.

Caucasian women: As noted above, Caucasian women have the highest incidence of negative body image and eating disorders. Part of the reason for this is, while the media tends to elevate Caucasian female features as the highest standard of beauty, the average woman simply can't live up to the Hollywood ideal. Unlike other ethnicities, white women who can't achieve the Hollywood standard have no cultural safety net to tell them that, even if they don't measure up to certain external standards, they can still be beautiful.

Hispanic women: Many Hispanic women complain that they are objectified by the male-dominated Spanish-language media, and many also feel that Hispanic men have unrealistic expectations for how women should look. In general, the men want women to be curvy, big-breasted and round-hipped, while also being skinny—a practically impossible goal for most women. There's also a perception in many Latin American countries that lighter skin, blonder hair and greater height correspond to being upper-class, educated and European. These nearly impossible expectations leave many Hispanic women feeling less than beautiful. And the fact that Latin American culture is, in many ways, highly sexualized and free can compound negative feelings for women with body image problems.

Asian-American women: The situation of Asian-American women is quite different. Although it varies depending on country of origin, many Asian-American women are pulled in two different directions. Their parents' culture may expect women to be small, thin and conservative in dress, while U.S. standards of beauty encourage them to be taller, curvier, more colorful and more Americanized in appearance. Stories abound of Asian-American women undergoing surgeries

African American women have had to define their own standards of beauty throughout history. It has helped give them a relatively healthy self-image.

to make their eyes look European, to augment their busts or even to lengthen their legs. And when Asian-American women have the chance to visit Asian countries, they often feel they stand out among local women, sometimes negatively, which can complicate body image feelings even further.

Cultural Overhaul Needed

Realistically, to change the growing trend of negative body image and eating disorders in women of all ethnic groups would require widespread, conscious cultural change, which is difficult. What can happen is for women to start reevaluating their attitudes about beauty and body shape on an individual basis. And if enough women find ways to empower themselves and to push back against restrictive views of beauty, maybe it will start a grassroots movement.

It can be hard to counter the media-driven image of beauty, especially when so many people, both men and women, seem to buy into it. But by exploring your own cultural heritage and embracing nonmainstream or more expansive versions of beauty, you can do your part for women everywhere.

Most importantly, don't worry about what other people think. Rather than letting other people's versions of beauty shape how you view yourself, set yourself up as a unique example of beauty. Find ways to have confidence in who you are, and you'll begin to set your own standard of beauty.

EVALUATING THE AUTHOR'S ARGUMENTS:

In this viewpoint the Montecatini Eating Disorder Treatment Center uses facts, statistics, examples, and reasoning to make the argument that body image problems affect women of all cultures and ethnicities. The author does not, however, use any quotations to support its point. If you were to rewrite this article and insert quotations, what authorities might you quote from? Where would you place quotations, and why?

Chapter 2

What Factors Contribute to Negative Body Image?

Body image controversies have revolved around the Barbie doll since it was first introduced in the 1960s.

False Beauty in Advertising and the Pressure to Look "Good"

"While the vast majority of people know that advertising images are enhanced and are an impossible dream, it still hurts."

Jo Swinson

In the following viewpoint Jo Swinson argues that digitally manipulated images in magazines and advertisements threaten people's body images. She discusses how advertisers routinely use Photoshop and other programs to airbrush photos. Digital enhancements include erasing wrinkles, smoothing skin, removing portions of waists and hips, and otherwise making already beautiful models and actresses even more visually perfect. Viewing this impossible beauty depresses people, says Swinson. Even when they know images have been touched up, their body image and self-confidence still take a hit. She concludes that advertisers must be held accountable for distributing images that are impossible to live up to in real life.

Swinson is a member of the British parliament and cofounder of the Campaign for Body Confidence.

1. What would a third of women sacrifice in order to look "ideal," according to Swinson?
2. What does the author say about actress Julia Roberts and model Christy Turlington?
3. What could L'Oreal not prove about one of its products, according to Swinson?

(CNN)–from smoothing skin and erasing wrinkles to enlarging muscles and slimming waists, airbrushing, or "photoshopping," men and women to so-called perfection is the norm in advertising. These images don't reflect reality, yet from a younger and younger age, people are aspiring to these biologically impossible ideals.

For some, the desire to look as perfect as these models can become all-consuming, and a wealth of evidence suggests that people in the UK are experiencing serious body image problems—a trend undoubtedly replicated around the globe. People unhappy about their bodies can develop eating disorders, turn to diet pills or steroids, or try cosmetic surgery and Botox injections.

One study found that one in four people is depressed about their body, another found that almost a third of women say they would sacrifice a year of life to achieve the ideal body weight and shape, and almost half of girls in a recent survey think the pressure to look good is the worst part of being female.

These very real and serious issues are not helped by the impossible visions of perfection everywhere in our visual culture. A growing body of scientific evidence reinforces the link between negative body image and exposure to idealized images.

Last year, I presented a portfolio of 172 studies to the Advertising Standards Authority, the industry watchdog in the UK. Many of these studies show that over the long term, viewing pictures of these "perfect" bodies leads to severe pressures in adults and, increasingly, children. One study reported on girls aged 5 to 7 who, when exposed to images of thin dolls like Barbie, said they wanted to

"Wow, Ed! You look so much younger! Cosmetic surgery?" "No. Digital enhancement!," cartoon by Bradford Veley, www.CartoonStock.com. Copyright © by Bradford Veley. Reproduction rights obtainable from www .CartoonStock.com.

look thinner compared with those who saw dolls with a healthier body shape.

From children's toys to TV programs, images of the idealized body have permeated every level of our visual culture.

This is why I brought the Lancôme ads for foundation makeup featuring Julia Roberts and Christy Turlington to the attention of the Advertising Standards Authority, which banned them for being misleading. They are prime examples of how the advertising media have distorted our perception of beauty.

From children's toys to TV programs, images of the "ideal" body have permeated every level of our visual culture. Both Turlington and Roberts are naturally beautiful, and neither of the two women needs digital retouching to look great. Yet both images were manipulated to the extent that L'Oreal, which owns Lancome, could not prove the makeup's ability to replicate such flawlessness.

Of course, people aren't blind to this issue—but while the vast majority of people know that advertising images are enhanced and are an impossible dream, it still hurts. The pressure to conform to such narrow ideals is overwhelming. Among the industry, there is a real fear of confronting reality: Even the Advertising Standards Authority wasn't allowed to see a pre-production photo of Roberts because of contractual arrangements.

The ban on these two advertisements sent a strong message to the industry to reflect on their practices, but of course more honesty and transparency in advertising is just one part of the wider battle to change our culture of perfection. Having recognized the urgent need to address growing body dissatisfaction in the UK, now-government Minister for Equalities Lynne Featherstone and I launched the Campaign for Body Confidence in March 2010.

Since then, we have been raising the profile of the body confidence agenda and furthering our belief that everyone has the right, whatever their size, shape or form, to feel happy about themselves. A diversity of body shapes and sizes needs to be included in magazines, advertising and broadcasts and on the catwalk—something our campaign partners All Walks Beyond the Catwalk have successfully been promoting.

FAST FACT

According to the nonprofit Social Issues Resource Centre, the ideal body type promoted in most advertisements is possessed naturally by fewer than 5 percent of females.

Equally a priority is the move away from our appearance-obsessed culture toward giving children positive examples of using their bodies, as well as bolstering their resilience and self-esteem with media literacy and body confidence lessons in schools.

British Parliament member Jo Swinson (pictured) believes that digitally manipulated images in the media negatively affect people's body images and self-confidence.

Though some people dismiss this issue as trivial, they are ignoring what is, in fact, a growing public health problem. It's vital that we take steps now so that members of the next generation will grow up learning to accept their bodies in a culture that celebrates health and confidence over a false ideal.

EVALUATING THE AUTHOR'S ARGUMENTS:

In this viewpoint Jo Swinson claims that advertisers should not be allowed to use technology to enhance photos unrealistically. How would Steven Thomson, author of the following viewpoint, specifically argue against this claim? With which author do you ultimately agree?

Digitally Manipulated Advertisements Should Be Embraced

"Artists have been idealizing the human form since antiquity. Did glorified visions of goddesses make young ancient Greek girls feel sorry for themselves?"

Steven Thomson

There is nothing wrong with digitally enhancing advertisements and photos, argues Steven Thomson in the following viewpoint. He likens such photos to art, saying that glorifying the human form has been a celebrated part of human culture for thousands of years. Thomson says people know the photos they see in ads and magazines are not real; thus, these images should not negatively affect them. In his view, perfect, flawless pictures are entertaining and help brighten an otherwise drab existence. He concludes that people who complain about digitally enhanced photos take them much too seriously.

Thomson is a former editor and writer for *CultureMap*, a publication based in Houston, Texas.

Steven Thomson, "Why Is Rachael Leigh Cook Up in (Flabby) Arms? In Defense of Airbrushing," *CultureMap Houston,* October 25, 2010.

G rocery shopping is hard: the bright lights, overeager air conditioning, rules prohibiting sampling jelly beans. So the last thing we need is to see too much junk in the trunk on a magazine cover in the checkout aisle. The bangin' bods, brushed up boobs and beautiful brows are a breath of fresh air during the daily grind of self-checkout loneliness.

All that would change if [actress] Rachael Leigh Cook has her way. Cook recently joined Geena Davis at the 2010 Healthy Media for the Youth Summit in Washington, D.C. for the Girl Scouts of the USA and The Creative Coalition to address body image issues for young girls.

"I think it's an absolute travesty that young women are seeing what the media is feeding them," Cook told Fox News on the subject of airbrushing. She continued:

"It breaks my heart to be part of an industry and part of a machine that really pushes out these images

FAST FACT

In 2011 researchers at Dartmouth College's Department of Science developed a software tool that can rate photographs based on how much they have been digitally altered.

and propagates these really terrible standards that are false. Nothing that you see is real, even if you look at what looks like a candid photo of someone, anything can be done. It is false advertising and false advertising is a crime, so why isn't this a crime? I'm just up in arms about it."

Advertisers Should Use the Tools That Sell

I hear that girls go through a lot of trouble reconciling media's idealized portrayal of women with their own bodies' self-worth. But on a basic level, it's a parent's responsibility to educate children about the

Actress Rachael Leigh Cook speaks at the Healthy Media for Youth Summit in Washington, D.C. Cook has been critical of the use of retouched photos by advertisers.

reality of celebrities depicted on magazines. Any adolescent is capable of understanding that the covers of *Cosmopolitan* and *People* are edited to resemble an unattainable level of beauty.

If we have the technology to create a more effective piece of advertising, the entertainment industry should capitalize on it. Would you not use a navigation device because it compromises your ability to learn how to read a paper map?

Just Another Form of Art
Utilizing airbrushed images can help an actor or model professionally, and the product in itself can be considered a craft—a point which Cook admits: "It's just all a complete illusion and maybe it should be

viewed as art, the way art isn't real. The way that a picture of a rose can be beautiful, but it's not a real rose."

Artists have been idealizing the human form since antiquity. Did glorified visions of goddesses make young ancient Greek girls feel sorry for themselves?

That Cook suggests airbrushing is an absolute crime even infringes on the notion of freedom of speech. But most importantly, should we be taking advice from a person whose career peaked with *The Babysitter's Club* and *She's All That?*

EVALUATING THE AUTHOR'S ARGUMENTS:

To make his argument, Steven Thomson likens airbrushed photos to paintings and other pieces of art. How do you think the other authors in this chapter would respond to this suggestion? Write one to two sentences on how you think each author might respond. Then, state your opinion—are such images a form of art? Why or why not?

UK Study Proposes Disclaimer for Airbrushed Models

Raphael G. Satter

"When girls evaluate themselves against unrealistic airbrushed images it cultivates a feeling of falling short, of not being 'good enough.'"

In the following viewpoint Raphael G. Satter discusses the British government's proposal to add a disclaimer to airbrushed ads. These disclaimers would warn consumers that the images of models are indeed too perfect, and let them know they have been digitally altered. The author suggests that when girls compare themselves to Photoshopped images, they feel inadequate and insecure. Such images contribute to negative body image, and thus the government has proposed placing limits on the extent to which such images may be modified without a consumer's knowledge.

Satter is a contributor to AP Online, an American news agency.

AS YOU READ, CONSIDER THE FOLLOWING QUESTIONS:

1. Describe the October 2009 Ralph Lauren ad that drew attention to the issue of Photoshopped images.
2. Who is Jo Swinson, and how does she factor into the author's argument?
3. According to the article, what might be the consequences of switching to models who are so perfect they do not need to be airbrushed?

London—A British government-commissioned study has proposed putting disclaimers on digitally altered images of models, warning consumers that the too-perfect woman staring at them from inside a fashion magazine is, in fact, too perfect.

But Britain's ad watchdog is cool to the proposal, and the publishing industry said more time was needed to unravel the matter.

Airbrushed ads and magazine covers not only set impossible standards of beauty but may also mislead people about the realities of their bodies.

"We still receive very, very few complaints on the airbrushing issue," Advertising Standards Agency spokesman Matt Wilson said, adding that his organization already had the power to act when airbrushed ads were offensive or misleading.

He noted that the agency had acted last year when an ad for Olay eye cream featuring supermodel Twiggy had the wrinkles around the 60-year-old's eyes removed electronically.

But as to the general issue of doctored photos, Wilson said that would be for the industry to decide.

The Periodical Publishers Association, which represents Britain's 6 billion pound ($9.1 billion) magazine and business media industry, said in a statement that more evidence was needed before deciding to start slapping disclaimers on photos, adding that the issue was "incredibly complex."

> **FAST FACT**
>
> In 2011 the American Medical Association adopted an anti-Photoshopping policy, saying that "exposure to media-propagated images of unrealistic body image [is linked] to eating disorders and other child and adolescent health problems."

The report, authored by psychologist and media personality Linda Papadopoulos, said that "when girls evaluate themselves against unrealistic airbrushed images it cultivates a feeling of falling short, of not being 'good enough.'"

She recommended that ratings should be affixed to such images to make clear if and how models had been altered.

The issue of airbrushing has arisen periodically in the U.K., and further attention was drawn to the issue in October when a model in a Ralph Lauren advertisement was so drastically photoshopped that her waist was left looking smaller than her head. Ralph Lauren said the image was displayed by mistake, but the freakish photo sparked outrage across the Internet.

Opposition Liberal Democrat lawmaker Jo Swinson has championed moves to force advertisers to post disclaimers that photos have been doctored, but the proposal has yet to become law.

Factors Influencing Girls' Body Image

A Girl Scout Research Institute study of teen and tween girls found that seven out of ten girls believe friends influence how they feel about their bodies, followed largely by family, fashion and media.

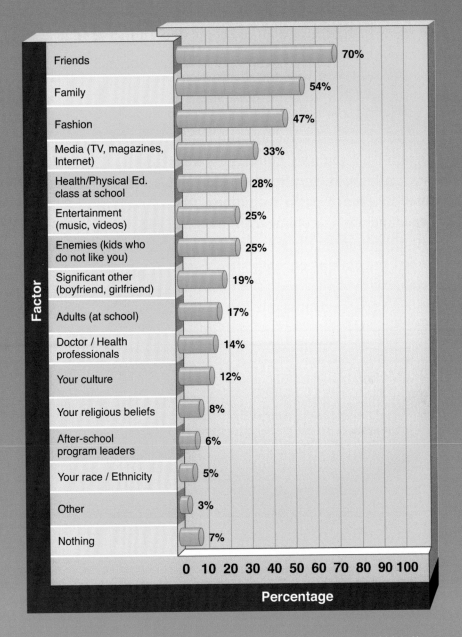

Factor	Percentage
Friends	70%
Family	54%
Fashion	47%
Media (TV, magazines, Internet)	33%
Health/Physical Ed. class at school	28%
Entertainment (music, videos)	25%
Enemies (kids who do not like you)	25%
Significant other (boyfriend, girlfriend)	19%
Adults (at school)	17%
Doctor / Health professionals	14%
Your culture	12%
Your religious beliefs	8%
After-school program leaders	6%
Your race / Ethnicity	5%
Other	3%
Nothing	7%

Taken from: Girl Scout Research Institute. Girl Survey Panel, April 2008. www.girlscouts.org/research/what_girls_say/body_image.asp.

Nevertheless, a steady stream of photoshopped advertisements—including an allegedly touched-up political poster featuring a particularly smooth-faced opposition British Conservative Party chief David Cameron—have kept the issue in the public eye.

London-area fashion photographer Paul Cable said he wouldn't be opposed to putting a disclaimer on doctored photos.

"To be fair, I don't think it will harm fashion photography or advertising," he said. "It just makes it clear to young kids that it has been retouched, because a lot of people don't understand it . . . and they might idolize the models."

But he cautioned that the disclaimers might lead advertisers to switch to models who don't need airbrushing—creating even more pressure on models to become thinner, by eating less, or to improve their figures with cosmetic surgery.

Britain isn't the only country to consider putting disclaimers on such ads—a tougher version of the proposed law also has been mooted by French parliamentarians.

Papadopoulos's recommendation on airbrushing is one of several aimed at countering the sexualization of children. Other proposals included restrictions on suggestive music videos, ways to combat pro-anorexia Web sites and tighter controls on racy men's magazines.

Britain's government said it was studying the report's advice.

EVALUATING THE AUTHOR'S ARGUMENTS:

Considering what you know about magazines, advertisements, digitally altered photos, and body image, what is your opinion of the British government's suggestion to put disclaimers on photos that have been altered? Would seeing such a disclaimer make you feel better about a too-perfect image? Would you worry that disclaimers would lead to the use of even more perfect models? Explain your opinion on this idea.

Consumers Enjoy the Fantasy of Enhanced Photos

Camilla Long

"Today's audiences are sophisticated enough to know the score and understand that they are buying a dream, not reality."

People realize and accept that photos are digitally enhanced, reports Camilla Long in the following viewpoint. She explains that retouching advertisements, photos, and other pieces of media has become a highly specialized and sophisticated process, one that can even be seen as a form of art. Humans have long altered the human form—busts, paintings, and statues have for hundreds of years projected an image of human beauty that has not necessarily reflected reality. Long suggests that people want to look at perfection, and that all aspects of life—including make-up, clothing, and other accessories—serve to enhance us. She reports the belief of many in the fashion industry who assert that customers know that photos are enhanced and prefer to see perfect, flawless images.

Long is a reporter for the *Sunday Times*, a London-based newspaper.

AS YOU READ, CONSIDER THE FOLLOWING QUESTIONS:
1. Who is Pascal Dangin, as reported by the author?
2. What does the phrase "digital knife" mean in the context of the viewpoint?
3. What does Long say the latest photo-enhancing technology is capable of doing?

Camilla Long, "The Master Manipulator," *Sunday Times*, May 18, 2008, p. 14.

Pascal Dangin, the "retouch" artist most sought by celebs, has sparked a debate on how far images are digitally altered Dove's "real women" advert, with Dangin's head digitally imposed on one of the women.

Inside an old warehouse in New York is a man who can make any woman beautiful. Sculpted cheekbones, slimmer waist, bigger bust or more smouldering eyes—Pascal Dangin can deliver them all.

Dangin is the master magician of "retouching" images by computer manipulation. He is sought out by top photographers such as Annie Leibovitz and Stephen Meisel and by film stars and models who seek perfection—or at least the impression of perfection.

In Dangin's world nothing is quite what it seems. Last week he let slip in a rare interview that he had tinkered with the Dove cosmetics campaign featuring "real women". Speaking to *The New Yorker* magazine, he was quoted as saying: "It was great to do, a challenge, to keep everyone's skin and faces showing the mileage but not looking unattractive."

Glossy magazines and advertising campaigns have long relied on the retoucher's skill and Dangin manipulates countless images for international editions of *Vogue* magazine. In the March issue of *US Vogue* alone, he digitally tweaked 107 advertisements, 36 fashion pictures and the cover image of Drew Barrymore.

However, the Dove case was different: the claim that he had applied his skills to a campaign whose very existence challenged the principles of retouching stirred controversy—as well as a denial from the company itself.

Dangin, said the company, had worked only on another of its campaigns, "Dove pro-age", helping merely with the "removal of dust from the film and minor color correction".

It added: "Dove strives to portray women by accurately depicting their shape, size, skin colour and age."

Nevertheless, the spat brought home the opposite point: these days almost everything goes under the digital knife and so skilful are retouchers such as Dangin that you will never see the scars.

Even Elizabeth Hurley, who recently revealed that she retouches her own holiday snaps, expressed astonishment at how widespread and comprehensive the practice has become. "The manipulation you can do," she said, "you can completely restructure a person."

Although artists of Dangin's calibre are prized for their subtlety, there are now almost no limits on what they can do thanks to the power of the latest technology.

Computers can banish wrinkles, slim down limbs and paint on make-up; they can plump up breasts, add volume to hair, fatten hips and enhance cleavage; they can remove cigarettes, tattoos or other items deemed unsuitable. They can even splice together facial features from separate images of the same person to create an ideal end product.

According to Dangin, the only public figure whose image tends not to be manipulated is the Queen.

Critics say that idealised images created by computers make for impossible role models. But if we know that every image is manipulated, does it matter? Are we not able to distinguish dream from reality?

Image manipulation has always gone on: in classical times, statues of emperors were created along ideal lines rather than any kind of verisimilitude. A bust of Julius Caesar found in the Rhône this week was unusual in that it portrayed the ageing military commander's wrinkles. Almost as soon as photography began, practitioners began manipulating prints.

The computer, argue some, has merely made the retoucher's art more sophisticated. Dangin recently demonstrated this with a photograph of a famous actress standing on a skyscraper.

First he shuffled the buildings behind her into a more pleasing arrangement and made the yellowy sky whiter. Then he fluffed out her dress with a "warping" tool.

He softened her collarbones, then thought that she looked a bit too retouched and made them bonier again.

He carefully left her crooked bottom row of teeth alone. "Her face is too high and elongated," he said. "But I don't want her to become someone else."

Dangin has been known to work for days trying to turn grass into the "most expressive" shade of green and cannot bear misaligned windows. Untruthful? Misleading?

"Humans have long colluded in an ideal of beauty," said Sally Brampton, the writer and former editor of *Elle*. Her first job was on *Vogue* in 1978 where she worked alongside two people dedicated solely to airbrushing images. "I am sure Helen of Troy was not that beautiful; we just buy into a collective ideal. Retouching is neither good nor bad: it is clearly something we want and until we decide we don't want it, it will remain that way."

So Kate Winslet's legs are lengthened, Penelope Cruz's eyelashes are thickened and Mariah Carey expresses an unashamed love of Photoshopping.

"Although you know it's cheating, it's gorgeous [to have it done]," admitted Tamara Beckwith, the party girl. "I did a job with Davina McCall to promote something and we both needed to wear white Wonderbras. She's quite busty and I'm not.

"But when I had a look at the pictures, suddenly I had this gorgeous cleavage. You want more and more."

Beckwith, however, is also wary of the influence on others. "Young people who don't have a clue about the fashion world may not understand," she said. "You can't sit there and pretend it's all good."

Indeed, the British Fashion Council was recently moved to warn magazine editors not to let retouching run out of control. Rosie Boycott, the former magazine and newspaper editor, goes further. "I don't agree with retouching, although I can see why it happens," she said. "I think it's fair enough when it comes to [removing] blemishes, but it gives people unattainable ideas of beauty.

"I don't like the whole way a star is presented to you: the package, the control.

It's just become an exercise in PR; retouching happens all the way through."

Juergen Teller, the photographer, who is renowned for not retouching his pictures, said: "I don't see a need for it; it's not what I find beautiful. Sometimes I am astonished. Beauty advertisers change everything and it doesn't do any good for the psyche of a woman."

On occasion retouching can deceive even celebrities as well as the public. There was an uproar when a magazine digitally removed Kylie

Minogue's knickers for one of its covers and Cat Deeley was horrified when she posed for a photo shoot only to discover later that most of her clothes had been erased.

Photography and fashion industry leaders claim that today's audiences are sophisticated enough to know the score and understand that they are buying a dream, not reality.

"A certain amount of retouching has always been a part of not only glossy magazines but all glamorous and celebrity-oriented material," said Alexandra Shulman, editor of *Vogue*. "We are not in the business of portraying reality all the time and people buy magazines like *Vogue* in order to look at a kind of perfection.

"They are sophisticated enough to know that what they are seeing is a construct. Nowadays people retouch their own snaps on the computer before posting them on Facebook."

Jeremy Langmead, editor of *Esquire* magazine, agreed. "Why shouldn't you look better? We strive to improve things in other areas of life, so if you have the technology it makes sense," he said. "If you don't like retouching you should also be against make-up. And if you want to know what real people look like, you can look out of the window."

A technician uses Photoshop to restore a badly damaged picture. The same techniques are used to enhance the beauty of models.

Teens Know Photos Are Touched Up

In 2010 a British website, the Good Surgeon Guide, conducted a scientific poll of more than one thousand teen girls. It found that the majority are aware that most celebrity images are airbrushed and not an accurate representation of the celebrities' appearances.

Are the majority of celebrity photos airbrushed and not an honest representation of their appearance?

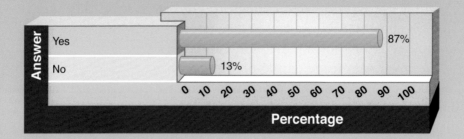

Which female celebrities are most often airbrushed?

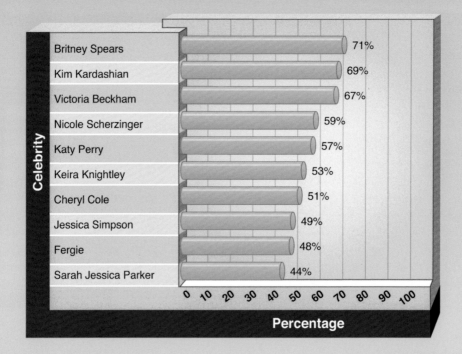

Taken from: "Teenage Girls Aspire to Look Like Airbrushed Celebrities." Good Surgeon Guide, 2010.
www.thegoodsurgeonguide.co.uk/press-releases/teenage-girls-aspire-to-look-like-airbrushed-celebrities~19/.

An all-too-stark reality check is also available in magazines such as *Heat* that specialise in photographs of stars caught unawares. Cellulite, lumpy clothes and pasty faces are all on display among Hollywood actors and models. Some publications even use digital trickery to emphasise these blemishes.

"We know it's not real, don't we," said Brampton. "My 16-year-old daughter accepts that the pictures are fake. She'll measure herself up to it but not in a damaging way. We fret about teenagers, but they are quite robust and cynical."

The art of digital manipulation has even come to be regarded with a humorous vanity. That was the reaction of Rachel Johnson, the writer, who was recently photographed for *Tatler*. "I was very cross," she said. "I wasn't retouched! I specifically said, 'I hope you're going to do lots of retouching', but I opened up the magazine and it was warts and all. Yellow teeth, red eyes and thunder thighs. I looked worse than [London socialite] Henry Conway, who was in the same issue."

Retouching is not always aimed at making women thinner. Fashion insiders say editors often ask for pictures of models to be bulked up, rather than slimmed down, especially if a model has lost weight in between being selected for a shoot and working on the studio session. With thousands of pounds riding on a shoot, boney ankles are not allowed to get in the way of perfection.

As long as we know that we are operating in a Matrix-like parallel universe, the industry argues, retouching does no harm. Dangin said: "I look at life as retouching. Make-up and clothes are just an accessorisation of your being—they are just a transformation of what you want to look like."

EVALUATING THE AUTHOR'S ARGUMENTS:

Camilla Long quotes from several sources to support the points she makes in her viewpoint. Make a list of everyone she quotes, including their credentials and the nature of their comments. Then, analyze her sources; what specific points do they support? Pick the quote you found most persuasive. Why did you choose it? What did it lend to Long's report?

Barbie Is Bad for Body Image

Galia Slayen

"I put [my old size-double-zero skirt] on Barbie to serve as a reminder that the way Barbie looks, the way I once looked, is not healthy and is not 'normal.'"

Galia Slayen made a life-size Barbie doll to show that Barbie is bad for body image. In the following viewpoint she describes the process. She measured a Barbie doll and then replicated her dimensions on a real-life scale. What she found was shocking: Her life-size Barbie was an imbalanced, gangly, big-chested freak. Slayen says that as a child, she was very taken with Barbie's perfection—so much so that over time, she developed poor body image and eventually an eating disorder. Dressing her life-size Barbie in the clothes she wore at the height of her eating disorder made her realize just how unhealthy and abnormal Barbie is. Each year, she brings her life-size Barbie around the country to show people how the doll contributes to a serious, life-threatening problem.

Slayen was a student at Hamilton College when this viewpoint was originally published.

AS YOU READ, CONSIDER THE FOLLOWING QUESTIONS:

1. What are Barbie's life-size measurements, according to Slayen?
2. When did the author create her life-size Barbie doll?
3. How many Barbie dolls are sold around the world every second, according to Slayen?

Galia Slayen, "The Scary Reality of a Real-Life Barbie Doll," HuffingtonPost.com, April 8, 2011. http://www.huffingtonpost.com.

Some people have skeletons in their closet. I have an enormous Barbie in mine.

She stands about six feet tall with a 39" bust, 18" waist, and 33" hips. These are the supposed measurements of Barbie if she were a real person. I built her as a part of the first National Eating Disorder Awareness Week (NEDAW) at my high school, later introducing her to Hamilton College during its first NEDAW in 2011.

Fond Memories, Bad Body Image

When I was a little girl, I played with my Barbie in her playhouse, sending her and Ken on dates that always ended with a goodnight kiss. I had fond times with my Barbie, and I admired her perfect blonde locks and slim figure. Barbie represented beauty, perfection and the ideal for young girls around the world. At least, as a seven-year-old, that is what she was to me.

In January 2007, I was looking for a way to make my peers realize the importance of eating disorders and body image issues. I was frustrated after quitting the cheerleading squad, frustrated with pressures to look and act a certain way and most of all frustrated with the eating disorder controlling my life. I wanted to do something that would turn others' apathy into action. That evening, my neighbor and I found two long pieces of wood and started measuring. With a little math, nails and hammering, we built a stick figure that stood about six feet tall.

> **FAST FACT**
>
> The National Eating Disorders Association reports that at five feet nine inches tall and weighing 110 pounds, Barbie would have a body mass index (BMI) of 16.24 and fit the criteria for anorexia. She likely would not menstruate and would be so out of proportion, she would have to walk on all fours.

The chicken wire came next. Surrounding her wooden frame, we created a body that wasn't much thicker than a stick figure, but had the womanly and unattainable curves and proportions that impressionable young girls idealize. We stuffed the chicken wire with newspaper and created a body that creepily leaned against the wall in my neighbor's

The Majority of Girls Own a Barbie Doll

Mattel, the company that makes Barbie, estimates that 90 percent of all American girls between the ages of 3 and 10 own at least one of its dolls. Those between 3 and 6 years of age are believed to own about twelve dolls each.

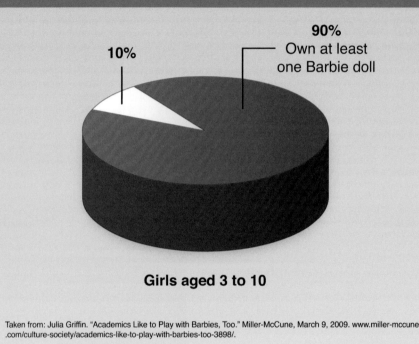

10%

90%
Own at least
one Barbie doll

Girls aged 3 to 10

Taken from: Julia Griffin. "Academics Like to Play with Barbies, Too." Miller-McCune, March 9, 2009. www.miller-mccune .com/culture-society/academics-like-to-play-with-barbies-too-3898/.

basement. She now needed some skin, so I brought her back to my apartment and employed the masterful art of papier maché.

Life-Size Barbie Is a Freak

Taking stacks of newspaper, glue and water, I skipped my high school semi-formal dance to give my girl some skin. Oddly, I started to feel my fondness for Barbie return, now not as a plaything but as a tool to reveal the negative body image that she promotes. As I papier machéd, I couldn't forget Barbie's impressive bust and blew up balloons over and over again to achieve a perfect 39" measurement. Once her chest was secured, I spent hours dipping and smoothing the paper, and later mixed paints to replicate her seemingly perfect white skin tone. With a little hard work and a lot of time, a headless, footless and handless body soon stood in my apartment.

But it was then I became stumped. I couldn't figure out how to recreate the recognizable face of the Barbie we all know and love. With NEDAW just around the corner, I was panicked. On my way to get office supplies, I drove by a Toys 'R' Us, and that's when it hit me. Remember that Barbie with just shoulders and a head, meant for you to practice brushing her hair? I confidently walked into the toy store for the first time since I was a kid. I found the Barbie head, found a friend to assemble that head, and clothed Barbie for her first debut.

A Scary Reminder

I dressed Barbie in my old clothes. The skirt she still has on today is a reminder of who I once was. That skirt, a size double zero, used to slip off my waist when I was struggling with anorexia. I put it on Barbie to serve as a reminder that the way Barbie looks, the way I once looked, is not healthy and is not "normal," whatever normal might mean. My Barbie's role is simple. She grabs the attention of apathetic onlookers and makes them think and talk about an issue that thrives in silence. In the last four years, Barbie has surpassed my expectations, attracting attention and sparking conversation among listeners and readers across the nation.

Once a year, at the end of February, Barbie comes out of the closet to meet my friends, strangers, and those apathetic onlookers. During NEDAW, she reminds people that eating disorders and body image issues are serious and prevalent. Holding an awareness week in high school or college is just one way to get students to discuss these important issues. However, constant discussion and education is key to dealing with and overcoming eating disorders.

Barbie and the Absurdity of Perfection

Despite her bizarre appearance, Barbie provides something that many advocacy efforts lack. She reminds [us] of something we once loved, while showing us the absurdity of our obsession with perfection.

- There are two Barbie dolls sold every second in the world.
- The target market for Barbie doll sales is young girls ages 3–12 years of age.

If the Barbie doll's measurements were of a life-size person, her body proportions would be completely unattainable for real women.

- A girl usually has her first Barbie by age 3, and collects a total of seven dolls during her childhood.
- Over a billion dollars worth of Barbie dolls and accessories were sold in 1993, making this doll big business and one of the top 10 toys sold.
- If Barbie were an actual woman, she would be 5'9" tall, have a 39" bust, an 18" waist, 33" hips and a size 3 shoe.
- Barbie calls this a "full figure" and likes her weight at 110 lbs.

- At 5'9" tall and weighing 110 lbs, Barbie would have a BMI [body mass index] of 16.24 and fit the weight criteria for anorexia. She likely would not menstruate.
- If Barbie was a real woman, she'd have to walk on all fours due to her proportions.
- Slumber Party Barbie was introduced in 1965 and came with a bathroom scale permanently set at 110 lbs with a book entitled "How to Lose Weight" with directions inside stating simply "Don't eat."

EVALUATING THE AUTHOR'S ARGUMENTS:

In this viewpoint Galia Slayen says her experience with Barbie led her to develop a poor body image and a dangerous eating disorder. In the following viewpoint Marjorie Cortez says that her experience playing with Barbie-type dolls was positive and imaginative. After reading both viewpoints, which author's experience resonates with you more? Why? List one piece of evidence or one quote that particularly struck you.

Viewpoint

6

Barbie Is Not Bad for Body Image

Marjorie Cortez

"Do I feel damaged by my childhood flirtation with Barbie? Not in the slightest."

Barbie does not negatively influence girls, argues Marjorie Cortez in the following viewpoint. She says there is little that is threatening or harmful about playing dress-up with dolls and fantasizing about their dates and weddings. She points out that the overwhelming majority of American girls own a Barbie, yet very few girls—about 5 percent—will develop an eating disorder. Cortez says that girls know Barbie is not supposed to be a model for real life. She believes they are more likely to model themselves after the more influential women in their lives, such as their mothers, coaches, and teachers.

Cortez writes editorials for the *Deseret News*, a Salt Lake City, Utah, newspaper.

AS YOU READ, CONSIDER THE FOLLOWING QUESTIONS:

1. What popular television series does Cortez say closely resembles the world of Barbie?
2. What percentage of American girls does the author say own at least one Barbie?
3. What, according to Cortez, was Barbie originally invented to represent?

Marjorie Cortez, "Girls Know Barbie Isn't a Role Model for Real Life," *Deseret News,* March 10, 2009.

B arbie's old enough for an AARP [American Association of Retired Persons] membership [i.e., fifty years old]. How weird is that? And so, for the umpteenth time, debates are raging on whether Barbie is a good role model for young girls.

Millions of girls have played with Barbie dolls for 50 years now. They've dressed them in fancy gowns, performed countless weddings between Barbie and Ken, and taken Barbie and friends on a few billion spins in pink Barbie convertibles. Best I can tell, it's all been good clean fun.

Although millions of girls have played with Barbie dolls, only a tiny percentage of them have developed poor body images, says the author.

Good Clean Fun

Who doesn't want to play dress up and live in a world where you always have matching shoes, handbags and other accessories? (Sounds suspiciously like the hit HBO series "Sex and the City," doesn't it?) Such play does not portend that you will have poor body images, self-esteem issues or preen about town in a Bob Mackie–designed gown.

That said, I never owned a true Barbie. I had a Barbie doll based on the actress Diahann Carroll. As a child, I was a fan of her television program "Julia." She was a single mom, nurse and a Vietnam war widow. She was one of the first African-American women on television not relegated to the role of a domestic worker. She had it going on. Besides, the doll talked!

My other Barbie was Skipper, a kid sister to Barbie. I remember performing a wedding ceremony between her and my brother's GI Joe, who had some impressive accessories of his own—an Apollo capsule and a complete astronaut outfit. Considering that NASA [National Aeronautics and Space Administration] astronauts were major heroes in my youth, Skipper could not have had a better suitor. Malibu Ken vs. GI Joe? No contest.

FAST FACT

The toy company Mattel reports that since her creation in 1959, Barbie has represented fifty nationalities and had 108 careers, many of which require a bachelor's degree or higher.

Barbie Did Not Harm Me

Do I feel damaged by my childhood flirtation with Barbie? Not in the slightest. When you come to realize that Barbie would be over 7 feet tall and weigh just 102 pounds if her proportions were human, it's a little difficult to think of her as the "ideal." It's more like a freak of nature.

The only woman I've ever seen in person who was that tall was former Utah Starzz center Margo Dydek. She's 7 foot 2 inches and weighs about 223 pounds, according to a WNBA [Women's National Basketball Association] Web site. Barbie only wishes she could block shots the way Margo can.

The Barbie phase for most girls is short-lived. As a parent, I was grateful for that because I grew tired of picking up Barbie's little acces-

Barbie Has Had Many Careers

According to a *Vogue UK* article, Barbie has had more than 100 careers since she was first invented in 1959. Some argue this makes her a ... role model for young girls. These jobs have included:

Year	Career
1960	Fashion designer
1961	Stewardess, nurse, ballerina, singer
1963	Career girl
1965	Astronaut
1973	Surgeon
1974	Miss America
1976	Ballet dancer, gold medalist
1977	Fashion model
1980	CEO of a company
1989	Unicef Barbie
1991	Air force Barbie
1993	Army Barbie
1996	Gymnast, veterinarian
1997	Dentist
2002	Art teacher
2004	Candidate for president
2005	TV producer, TV celebrity chef
2010	Computer engineer, news anchor, doctor, race car driver, rock star, snowboarder

Taken from: Lauren Milligan. "Barbie Works." *Vogue (UK)*, May 19, 2010. www.vogue.co.uk/news/2010/05/19/barbies-careers-and-jobs.

...ries. They had this uncanny way of ending up underfoot whe... ...umbled around in the dark to comfort a child who was ill or w... ...d had a bad dream. It was rather a relief when my daughters' int... ...s changed.

What Factors Contribute to Negative Body Image?

Neither of them turned into a Barbie. Nor, I suspect, will the 90 percent of American girls ages 3 to 10 who own at least one Barbie, according to Mattel's statistics.

Girls Have More Influential Role Models

The reason is, girls are not solely influenced by the likes of Barbie. Most girls have strong female role models in their mothers, their grandmothers, aunts and other women in their sphere of influence, such as coaches, Sunday School teachers or community leaders.

My daughters, now teenagers, live in a time when women have every opportunity and choice to be whatever and whoever they want.

To hear Barbie's inventor tell it, that's what she intended Barbie to represent, a young woman with choices. Isn't that what we, as mothers, want for our daughters?

EVALUATING THE AUTHOR'S ARGUMENTS:

To make her argument, Marjorie Cortez points out that millions of girls have played with Barbie, yet only a tiny percentage of them have developed poor body image or an eating disorder. Do you think this proves that Barbie is not bad for body image? Why or why not? Explain your reasoning using evidence from the texts you have read.

Viewpoint 7

Corporations Promote Body Image Anxieties to Sell Products

Libby Copeland

"In advertising terms, ... you don't sell the product, you sell the need."

In the following viewpoint Libby Copeland explains how advertisers create body image anxieties in order to sell their products. She documents how, for decades, corporations have made women feel bad about parts or aspects of their body, pushing problems that most did not even know existed. Once they feel bad about themselves, says Copeland, women are more likely to buy a product that they think will make them feel better. Copeland explains how companies have made women feel self-conscious about their bad breath, smelly armpits, and other natural issues, precisely so they are able to sell them billions of dollars of products. In some cases these products have been needless; in others, they have actually threatened women's health. Copeland concludes it is immoral for companies to create and prey on women's insecurities to make profits.

Copeland is a staff writer for the *Washington Post*. Her articles have also appeared in the *National Post* and on Slate.com.

AS YOU READ, CONSIDER THE FOLLOWING QUESTIONS:
1. What is the Dove Ultimate Go Sleeveless campaign, as reported by Copeland?
2. How did a 1953 toothpaste ad prey on women's insecurities, according to the author?
3. What company popularized the phrase "often a bridesmaid but never a bride?" according to Copeland?

Dove recently unveiled its latest campaign, and it hinges on the idea that your armpits are ugly. Dove Ultimate Go Sleeveless is supposed to give women "softer, smoother underarms in just five days"—in ads for the product, which [comic] Stephen Colbert calls a "breakthrough shame-o-vation," women cut the sleeves off their tops with joyful expressions, as if they've been liberated from a terrible scourge. If it's news to you that this part of your body is not so hot, Dove says you're in the minority, citing a survey in which 93 percent of women said they "think their underarms are unattractive." And if you doubt statistics culled from 534 women in an anonymous online poll, rest assured that Dove's best advertising efforts will be directed at making those numbers true.

Creating Anxiety to Sell the Cure

Pity the poor deodorant-makers. What else are they to do? As the *Wall Street Journal* points out, they're in a bind—almost the entire U.S. population already uses deodorant, and consumers appear reluctant to switch to new brands. Dove's empowerment-via-shame marketing approach for Go Sleeveless has its roots in advertising techniques that gained popularity in the 1920s: a) pinpoint a problem, perhaps one consumers didn't even know they had; b) exacerbate anxiety around the problem; c) sell the cure.

The history of ads directed at women is particularly rich with such fear tactics. Thus, ad copy from the 1920s and '30s warned women of their place in the "beauty contest of life" (a corset manufacturer) and reminded them that "The Eyes of Men . . . The Eyes of Women/ Judge your Loveliness every day" (Camay soap). A 1953 ad for Chlorodent toothpaste stated point-blank: "There's another woman waiting for every man." Yikes!

"In advertising terms," writes historian James B. Twitchell in *Twenty Ads That Shook the World,* "you don't sell the product, you sell the need."

Herewith, a brief history of our ugliest body parts, as recounted by the advertising industry:

How the Problem of Bad Breath Was Marketed

The substance that became Listerine was first invented in the late 19th century for use as a surgical antiseptic. In the 1920s, looking to goose sales, Gerard Lambert, son of the company's founder, began casting about for other uses for the product. As Stephen Fox writes in *The Mirror Makers: A History of American Advertising and Its Creators,* Lambert consulted a chemist and discovered that the product could be used for bad breath. Ad copy adopted the term *halitosis* "as a sober, medical-sounding way of referring to the unmentionable," Fox writes. Using a technique Fox calls "advertising by fear," the copy for Listerine [ads] suggested that consumers could have bad breath without knowing it, since even their closest friends might not tell them.

Listerine targeted men and women, but the phrase "often a brides-maid but never a bride" was made famous by the company's ads. In one 1925 image, a woman reads another woman's wedding announcement with a troubled expression on her face. "Her case was really a pathetic one," the copy intones, describing the woman as nowhere near marriage "as her birthdays crept gradually toward that tragic thirty mark." The culprit? Halitosis, of course.

"It's hard to assess Lambert's genius fairly," writes Twitchell in *Twenty Ads.* "It looks so easy, but it was a combination of staking a claim on a body part, knowing how to use constructive discontent (shame) as a selling tool, of realizing the power of research, and then of hammering it home."

Of course, it's not that people's breath didn't smell before, Twitchell points out—rather, "it was not considered socially offensive." Listerine changed that, creating both the problem and its cure.

The author says Dove's Go Sleeveless campaign is a shameless attempt to get women to switch to Dove deodorant.

Romance and Rejection

Odorono wasn't the first commercial deodorant in the U.S., but it played a role in the delicate art of marketing the "unmentionable." As historian Juliann Sivulka has written in a paper on deodorant advertising, this particular brand of "toilet water for perspiration" first began to take off in the 1910s. The company had some success with more traditional types of advertising—small print ads emphasizing the safety and efficacy of the product, which was then primarily marketed to women. But its sales pla-teaued, and when the company's ad agency conducted home surveys it discovered that many nonusers considered Odorono a product for other women, those with serious perspiration problems, not for themselves.

This is when the advertisers tried something new. Combining the promise of romance with the horror of rejection, a full-page ad in a 1919 issue of *Ladies' Home Journal* offered the image of a man and woman about to embrace. The copy explained that "fastidious women who want to be absolutely sure of their daintiness have found that they could not trust to their own consciousness," because "it is a physiological fact that persons troubled with perspiration odor seldom can detect it themselves."

Could the reader be absolutely sure she didn't smell, even just once in a while—maybe at precisely the wrong moment, in a moonlight garden in the arms of her lover? Or, as the ad put it, "Would you be absolutely sure of your daintiness?" With a few precise jabs at the readers' insecurities, the ad transformed Odorono "from a proprietary medicine to a beauty aid," Sivulka writes, shifting "an unmentionable topic to one of primary importance to every woman."

A Dangerous and Ineffective "Cure"

Down there is its own continent, and over the decades a myriad of marketing strategies have arisen to conquer it. The book *Flow* has chronicled the challenges of selling menstruation products without offending the delicate sensibilities of the American consumers. But pads and tampons are not the only corner of the feminine hygiene market that has been cloaked in euphemism. Consider douches and feminine deodorants, which offered the promise of what ads have labeled "intimate daintiness."

From the 1930s through the 1960s, according to Andrea Tone's *Devices and Desires*, the top feminine hygiene product in the country was Lysol. In addition to being marketed as a mouth gargle, a household cleaner, and more, the disinfectant was sold as a douche. Consumers understood that Lysol douche was to be used as a contraceptive, Tone writes, although the ads used veiled language, alluding to problems like

> **FAST FACT**
>
> A 2010 study published in the *Journal of Consumer Research* found that ads featuring beauty products lowered female consumers' self-esteem by a statistically significant amount.

"germs" and "odors," and suggesting that a wife's "fear of a major crisis" (code for becoming pregnant) could lead to marital discord and divorce. The ads tended to lay the happiness of the marriage—and the power to limit family size—squarely in the woman's lap. Only the "proved germicidal efficiency of Lysol" can "restore every woman's confidence in her power to please," one 1948 ad declared.

A poll conducted jointly by *Fitness* magazine and ICR/International Communications Research asked over one thousand men and women the following questions related to body image and appearance.

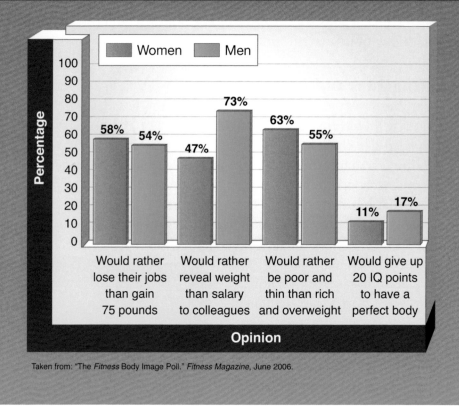

Taken from: "The *Fitness* Body Image Poll." *Fitness Magazine*, June 2006.

The unfortunate truth was that as a contraceptive, Lysol was ineffective, not to mention dangerous. Improperly diluted, it burned and blistered the vagina, and in some cases even caused death. Yet, Tone writes, it wasn't until the pill came along that Lysol douche was supplanted as the top choice of women looking to prevent pregnancy.

Women Have More Serious Problems

In the '60s, ads for feminine deodorant sprays and feminine wipes continued with the theme of troublesome odor, but without the double meaning. In her brilliant 1973 *Esquire* piece on feminine hygiene sprays, Nora Ephron traced how marketers surfed the wave of the sexual revolution to sell a product that, if anything, ran counter to the idea of liberated sexuality. Like Lysol douche, products such as FDS, Massengill Powder, and Bidette Mist at once aroused anxiety about women's vaginas and offered solutions to the problem.

Ephron quotes a 1968 ad for FDS posing the question of whether women need more than underarm deodorant. "Yes," the ad helpfully answers itself. "A woman, if she's completely honest about it, realizes her most serious problem isn't under her arms."

Well, the makers of Dove Ultimate Go Sleeveless might beg to differ.

EVALUATING THE AUTHOR'S ARGUMENTS:

Libby Copeland argues that advertisers encourage people to feel bad about their bodies so they will buy products to fix themselves. Think about the way you buy products. Are any of them intended to "fix" parts of yourself? If so, what products, and what parts? Write one to two paragraphs in which you reflect on the way in which advertisements make you feel, and how that factors into your decision to buy a product.

Chapter 3

How Can Body Image Be Improved?

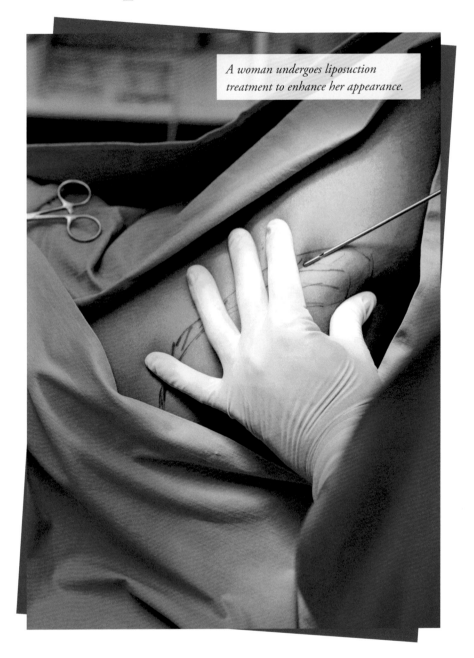

A woman undergoes liposuction treatment to enhance her appearance.

Size-Zero Models Should Be Discouraged

Kira Cochrane

"The images of women that are multiplying around us look not just unhealthy, but in some cases horrifying."

In the following viewpoint Kira Cochrane warns that ultra-skinny models promote unhealthy, even horrifying, body standards. She explains that for a brief time, the fashion industry embraced larger models that reflected a healthier, more normal body type. But in recent years, super-skinny size-size 0 models have returned to the catwalk. In Cochrane's opinion, extremely thin models not only offer horrifying visions of gaunt eyes and jutting bones; they also glorify a lifestyle that can result in death. For all of these reasons, she thinks size 0 models should be discouraged from the fashion and advertising industries.

Cochrane is a features writer for the *Manchester Guardian,* a British newspaper.

AS YOU READ, CONSIDER THE FOLLOWING QUESTIONS:

1. Who are Hayley Morley and Crystal Renn, as cited by the author?
2. What killed models Luisel Ramos and Ana Carolin Reston, according to Cochrane?
3. What does the author think is not too much to ask of the fashion industry?

Kira Cochrane, "Why Are Models Still So Thin?," *The Guardian,* March 14, 2010.

Last year was supposed to have been the end of the super-thin supermodel. So why were the collarbones and hollow necks back on the catwalk again at this year's shows?

In 2009, as the leaves turned orange, and autumn met winter, it seemed as though a new trend was taking hold in fashion. After year upon year of emaciated young women stalking the catwalks, a new breed was in the spotlight. These weren't the fetishised fat women we'd occasionally seen before—they didn't resemble Beth Ditto, naked, on the cover of *Love* magazine, her rolls of flesh beautiful, but much more bountiful, than any average woman's. They didn't signal the industry replacing one extreme body shape with another. Instead, they were that unlikely sight, a vision that made people double take. They were women with healthy, normal bodies.

Hayley Morley, a size 12, took to the catwalk for knitwear designer Mark Fast. Lizzie Miller, a size 14, caused a furore when pictured naked with a roll of stomach flesh in *US Glamour* magazine. And then there was the size 16 supermodel, Crystal Renn, who published her autobiography *Hungry*, and appeared in *Vogue*, *Glamour* and *V* magazine's Size Issue. Renn said that a new kind of model was emerging, "lush and sparkly with nary a jutting collarbone in sight".

Then came the latest round of autumn/winter ready-to-wear shows, which ended in Paris last week.

Jutting collarbones weren't just easy to spot; they were almost ubiquitous. There were the hollowed-out necks striped with taut, rope-like tendons, straining to keep balloon-like heads aloft on child-like shoulders. There were the tiny upper arms, fragile and snappable as a bird wing stripped of feathers. And, perhaps most notably, there were the women's thighs, space gaping between them, often even slimmer at their upper reaches than at the stark, bony knees. In some cases, it was hard to fathom how the women could walk. There were a couple of shows—Louis Vuitton and Prada—where healthier bodies were on

> ## FAST FACT
>
> A 2009 survey of a thousand women conducted by the Dove Campaign for Real Beauty found that 96 percent said they think models used in beauty advertising do not realistically represent women.

A size 0 model walks the catwalk at a fashion show. The author argues that such thin models promote an unhealthy lifestyle.

display. But they were the exceptions; and anyway they weren't a political statement, they were simply an aesthetic choice. Miucca Prada did put healthy women into that Prada show, but at her other show—her Miu Miu show—some of the models were skeletal.

Even designers from whom you might expect more, such as Stella McCartney—famous for designing trousers that real women can actually wear—put models on the catwalk who looked far too thin for comfort.

No one seems to have said a thing. After years of arguments about the extreme thinness of fashion models, after horror at the 2006 deaths of Luisel Ramos (who had fasted for several days), and Ana Carolina Reston (who died from an infection related to anorexia), after the editor of British *Vogue*, Alexandra Shulman, voiced her worries last year about models with "jutting bones and no breasts or hips", the debate seems to have gone eerily silent.

Many Models Have a Lower than Normal Body Mass Index

The body mass index (BMI) is an index based on weight and height. A BMI of between 18 and 25 is healthy and normal. Most models and actresses, however, have much lower BMIs.

Scale	Model / Actress	BMI
0–18 Underweight	Heidi Klum	18
18–25 Healthy weight	Gisele Bündchen	17.4
25–30 Overweight	Elle MacPherson	17.3
30+ Obese	Nicole Richie	17
	Paris Hilton	16
	Kate Moss	15.7
	Lily Cole	15.6
	Twiggy	14.7

It's not clear why. Perhaps it's that the existence of a few healthier women has acted as a diversion, has convinced the outside world that the industry is changing. Or perhaps it's just that we're tired of talking about it. After all, emaciated women have been a fixture in fashion for at least 15 years now, since the amazonian supermodels of the late 80s and early 90s—Cindy Crawford, Linda Evangelista, Naomi Campbell, Christy Turlington—made way for heroin chic and hollowed-out eyes, for an ideal of womanhood that has become thinner and thinner and thinner.

But it does seem important to point out that this is still going on, that the images of women that are multiplying around us look not just unhealthy, but in some cases horrifying. It's not that every woman on the catwalk has to be a certain size, not that they all need to be weighed at the door to the venue, but it would be a big leap forward if catwalk photographs didn't seem bound, instantly, for a pro-anorexia website. Surely that's not too much to ask?

EVALUATING THE AUTHOR'S ARGUMENTS:

In this viewpoint Kira Cochrane suggests that the fashion industry has a responsibility to promote healthy images of women. In the following viewpoint, Alexandra Shulman suggests that the fashion industry has a responsibility to make money, something that is best done by using skinny models. After reading both viewpoints with which author do you ultimately agree? Why? List at least one piece of evidence that swayed you.

Size-Zero Models Should Not Be Discouraged

Alexandra Shulman

"Discriminating against someone because of their body type, whether too fat or too thin, is surely something that should not be encouraged."

In the following viewpoint Alexandra Shulman argues that size 0 models should not be banned, nor should they be blamed for promoting unhealthy body image. She argues that discriminating against thin people is no different than discriminating against fat ones—in addition to opening up the fashion industry to lawsuits, it is wrong to discriminate against someone for their size. She also suggests that a model's size is not a true indication of her health—larger models might be unhealthier than naturally thin ones, according to Shulman. Finally, Shulman argues that it is not the job of the fashion industry to promote good health. The industry's primary purpose is to promote fantasy and sell clothes. She concludes that it is wrong to blame the fashion industry and size 0 models for promoting poor body image.

Shulman is the editor of British *Vogue* and a member of the British Fashion Council.

Alexandra Shulman, "Size Zero Hysteria at London Fashion Week," *The Daily Mail,* February 5, 2007.

1. What, according to Shulman, is similar to censoring art and literature?
2. What other professionals does the author sarcastically suggest should be tested for health, if models' health is to be scrutinized?
3. What does Shulman say would happen if magazine photo shoots used size 14 women?

During the recent Chanel couture show, I sat next to Erin O'Connor, the articulate and bony "face" of London Fashion Week as well as one of the popular models in the M&S advertising campaign.

As we waited for the show to begin, I asked her about how her involvement with London Fashion Week was going.

Fine, it was an interesting role, she answered, but she was incandescent with rage about how members of her industry were being victimised for their size.

She felt it appalling and patronising that these girls were being treated as if they were brainless pieces of meat, unable to think for themselves, with the suggestion that they should be weighed in like prize heifers.

Likewise, a few weeks earlier I spoke to Lily Cole, currently one of Britain's most successful international fashion models—incredibly thin, incredibly tall—helping to support her single mother and about to become a Cambridge under graduate.

She joined me at a debate on fashion and responsibility at the London College of Fashion, and she argued strongly that this criticism of her colleagues' body shape was extremely undermining—especially for the very young models (who, for the record, we agreed shouldn't be there in the first place) who are more vulnerable.

I was interested in the comments because OK, hands up, mea culpa, I am a member of the British Fashion Council—the very body which Liz Jones referred to last week in the pages of this paper as "a sickening, self-interested fashion conspiracy".

Right now that makes me about as warmly regarded in the pages of the national Press as a member of Opus Dei.

Well, let me argue my case.

The BFC is an organizing body responsible for the staging of London Fashion Week and includes representatives of my own

British Vogue *editor Alexandra Shulman (pictured) argues that discriminating against thin people is no different than discriminating against fat people.*

company, Conde Nast (which publishes *Vogue* and *Glamour*), alongside others—Tesco, Selfridges, Arcadia (home of Topshop and Wallis) and Debenhams.

Last week, this committee issued a statement detailing their current response to the so-called size zero debate, which included the fact that they were not prepared to ban skinny models.

The next thing we knew, headlines about the BFC's "refusal to ban" anybody or anything were scatted all over the place. Hence Liz's furious response.

Well, first things first: Size 0. I defy anyone to walk into any store in this country and find a size 0.

Size 0, like so many nifty phrases, is an import from the States. They—in an effort to flatter their citizens—label all their sizes smaller than we do.

For instance, a U.S. size 10 is a UK size 14-ish. (Sizes are not an exact science.)

That means that a size 0, if my maths are right, is equivalent to about size 4. Still jolly hard to find in the stores.

But it's that apocryphal size 0 that has captured the imagination.

In fact, before that phrase was imported, I don't believe the general public were very much engaged in this subject at all, so whoever introduced it has at least scored some kind of linguistic coup.

According to Liz Jones, the British Fashion Council refused to "ban" size 0 models because of a variety of reasons, which range from "putting big business before the health of young women in this country" to a fear of our "jobs, dress allowances, discounts and designer freebies".

Hmm. If I might be allowed to borrow from the immortal words of Sir Philip Green to me the other day, about a completely different person: "What's she been smoking, eh?"

I see no way in which this decision could have been made out of the assembled company's self-interest.

For many of us, our role is to create clothes and images that people want to buy. If we fail, then we are out of a job—and pretty quickly.

Stuart Rose, the chairman of the BFC didn't double the share price of M&S by catering to a few designers on the London catwalk.

And as for dress allowances and designer freebies, I doubt they flood into most of the offices of the BFC committee, such as Julia Reynolds at Tesco.

Admittedly they do come my way—but why should that influence what I feel about this issue? Why should I, as an editor of a magazine that sells primarily to women, want to deliberately sabotage the health of young women for the sake of a free handbag or several?

The London catwalk shows take place twice a year, with the aim of promoting the work of our independent and often struggling designers via images later used in newspapers, magazines, websites and TV around the world.

The British Fashion Council—and this is important—is not a legislative nor regulatory body.

They choose, via consultation with Press and buyers, which designers they will put on schedule, but their involvement with the shows generally stops there.

Consequently, our recent and mis-represented statement promises what we believe we can legitimately achieve, rather than some crowd-pleasing and yet utterly unrealistic soundbite proposal to silence the baying mob.

What we have said is this: "The BFC recognises its responsibility to help promote a healthy body image."

We have asked designers, model agencies and image-makers "to use only healthy models for their collections"; we accept a need for "the commitment of the fashion industry to change attitudes through behaviour and education".

FAST FACT

In 2011 researchers Davide Dragone and Luca Savorelli of the University of Bologna, Italy, reported data that suggested very skinny models motivate people to stay slim. They warned that increasing the size of fashion models would alter people's perception of ideal weight and in turn cause the general population to gain weight.

All are quotes from letters sent out last week.

What we haven't done is promise to ban skinny models. Why?

Gosh, where to begin? At this point I should stress that I am writing this not as a member of the BFC, since they won't have seen this piece, but as *Vogue*'s editor for 15 years and as a 49-year-old woman, mother and stepmother.

The BFC, like their counterparts the CFDA (Council of Fashion Designers of America) in New York, the Chambre Syndicale in Paris and the Camera Nazionale in Milan, have resisted the notion of pretending that they can keep girls with a BMI of less than 18 off the catwalk because, after a huge amount of discussion, they have agreed that it is not right to and they can't—in that order.

Discriminating against someone because of their body type, whether too fat or too thin, is surely something that should not be encouraged.

"Fashion Show," cartoon by Mike Keefe, *The Denver Post,* September 22, 2006, www.PoliticalCartoons.com. Copyright © 2006 by Mike Keefe, *The Denver Post,* and www.PoliticalCartoons.com.

Indeed, in these days of litigation I wouldn't be surprised if a model might not be able to sue for such behaviour.

Dictating to a creative industry exactly how they should show their work is also an alien concept—along the lines of censoring art and literature.

In its desire not to ban skinny models, but to do its very best to encourage designers to use girls who are not only healthy but appear to be, the British Fashion Council is going as far as it can.

And as for can't, even if the BFC did decide they thought it was a good idea to police the shows with an army of doctors wielding BMI measuring callipers, exactly how would they do it?

Designers do not have to tell the BFC which models they are using and probably don't make up their mind until the day before, so policing would have to take place then and there, with overly thin-looking girls hauled off at the end of the show to be banned from working.

And can it really be thought correct to suggest that models alone should carry a health certificate to practise their job?

Try measuring the liver function of any number of writers and journalists. Why don't we put a cholesterol limit on bankers and estate agents? How about a cardiac check on City traders?

The argument that seeing preternaturally thin models inspires young women to starve themselves in order to emulate these girls is a valid one.

Girls and boys (indeed, also grown women and men) who have an eating disorder look to the skeletally thin as idealised body images. They admire their contemporaries for starving; they hero-worship thin celebrities and models; they make starvation their life work.

It's a terrible life, and one that sometimes leads to death. But anorexia and bulimia are not confined to the catwalk.

You don't have to look far to find it in bank clerks, shop assistants and librarians, and their genesis cannot simply be blamed on fashion—tempting as it always is to pin the argument on a scapegoat.

We live in a society where, when we open our newspapers and magazines, as well as seeing pictures of thin celebrities, we see page after page of diets and attempted diets, followed by tales of sickening obesity. There's a whole genre of publishing that enjoys drawing red rings round any famous person's and every summer tabloid papers regularly run features on celebrity paunches and weight gain as they strut in Vilebrequin trunks and Gucci bikinis on the beach.

So to blame this situation solely on the fashion industry wildly over-exaggerates the influence that we have, and frankly credits us for innovations in cultural mores that owe their inception to a far greater range of issues than the London catwalk.

The important question is not a model's vital statistics but her health, both physical and mental.

That said, the whole issue of broadening the spectrum of body image role models is one which I welcome wholeheartedly and I've devoted six pages of the next issue of *Vogue* to the fashion industry and skinny models.

Frankly, I'd love my own size (14 on a bad day, 12 on a good) not to be an issue in every interview I do.

I believe that everything possible should be done to encourage young people to appreciate their bodies, whatever their size, and to judge themselves on a far broader range of criteria than how bit their bottom is.

Larger store mannequins sound like a good idea. Most High Street stores use dummies that fit a size 6 to size 10 and are usually taller than the average woman.

Big sample sizes would help. Certainly the proposed task force the

BFC is setting up with Tessa Jowell to look at instituting "a range of guidelines for the fashion industry as a whole" could be a good start.

As for the forthcoming London Fashion Week, if you see the odd image of a girl with gaping bandy legs and skinny arms in the papers, don't be surprised.

Picture desks are going to be scrutinizing the shows for them, since they are now a better story than models wearing something utterly ridiculous, like tin foil and space helmets.

Everything won't have changed overnight.

But in the midst of all this, it's important not to forget the wonderful, escapist, inspiring and enjoyable side of fashion that we all love.

Fashion shows and fashion photographs are there to show clothes in their best possible light and to make us dream of them and want to own them.

And, annoying as it is, the majority of us feel that clothes look better on slim women.

If I started to photograph all our shoots on size 14 women (and remember the camera lies—it piles on the pounds) would everyone want to look like them? I think not.

If we want to see how clothes look realistically, we don't have to peer at fashion magazines or catwalk pictures.

We can just look in the mirror.

EVALUATING THE AUTHOR'S ARGUMENTS:

Alexandra Shulman is a member of the fashion industry. She is the editor of an influential fashion magazine and sits on the British Fashion Council. In what way does knowing her background influence your opinion of her argument about size 0 models? Are you more likely to agree with her? Less likely? Why? Explain your reasoning.

Teens Choose Plastic Surgery to Boost Self-Esteem

"Thousands of [teens] are so deeply dissatisfied by what they see [in the mirror] that they try to permanently change the image reflected in the glass through plastic surgery."

Victoria Thompson

Victoria Thompson is a reporter for ABC News. In the following viewpoint she reports on how thousands of teen girls have chosen to get plastic surgery to boost their self-esteem. Tired of being teased for having big noses or small breasts, many opt to go under the knife to feel happier, more confident, and less shy. The author reports that some teens feel so emboldened by one procedure, they will opt to have a second procedure done. Unlike adults, who tend to have plastic surgery to set themselves apart, Thompson reports that teens opt to have surgeries they think will help them to better fit in.

Victoria Thompson, "Teens Choose Plastic Surgery to Boost Self-Esteem," *Nightline,* ABCnews.com, November 24, 2010.

1. How many plastic surgery procedures were performed on teens aged thirteen to nineteen in the United States in 2009, according to Thompson?
2. How many teens does the author report had nose jobs in 2009?
3. How many of the eight thousand thirteen- to nineteen-year-olds who had breast enlargements in 2009 were under eighteen, according to Thompson?

M ost teens love the mirror, spending hours in front of it experimenting with hairstyles, makeup and fashion. But thousands of them are so deeply dissatisfied by what they see each year that they try to permanently change the image reflected in the glass through plastic surgery.

"I have really low self-esteem," Caitlin Clemons, 18, said in the days before her breast augmentation surgery.

Watching her mother and sister gain confidence after undergoing their own breast enlargements convinced the Galveston, Texas, woman that the surgery could do the same for her.

"Once I saw how happy she was, I knew I could be that happy," Clemons said of her sister. "I'll have confidence. It definitely made me want the surgery more. Once my mother got hers and I saw it can be done, it really clicked in my mind that I can do this."

Nearly 210,000 cosmetic plastic surgery procedures were performed on people age 13 to 19 in 2009, according to the American Society of Plastic Surgeons. While adults tend to have plastic surgery to stand out from the crowd, teens tend to have surgery to change the parts of their body they believe are flawed so that they can fit in with their peers, experts say.

FAST FACT

The American Society of Plastic Surgeons reports that in 2010, approximately 219,000 cosmetic plastic surgery procedures were performed on Americans between thirteen and nineteen years old.

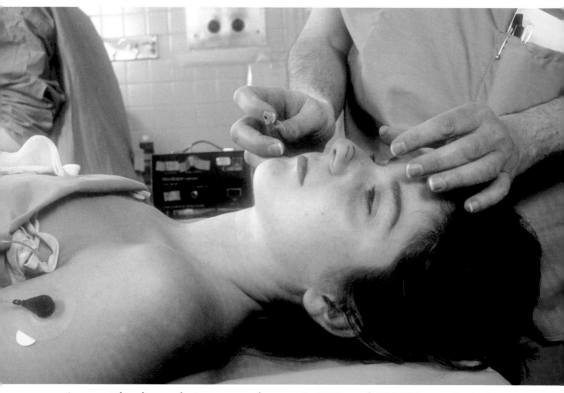

A young girl undergoes plastic surgery on her nose. In 2009 nearly 210,000 cosmetic plastic surgery procedures in the United States were performed on teens.

Clemons is no exception. "I have always been the friend with small breasts, unlike everyone else," she said. "I was tired of being teased about it. I've always judged myself. I've always looked at my friends, my sister and just kind of picked at myself, picked at my body and pulled out every imperfection that I could find."

The most popular procedure among teens is a nose job, also known as rhinoplasty. Nearly 35,000 U.S. teenagers had their noses surgically reshaped last year, according to the American Society of Plastic Surgeons.

Teens sometimes emboldened by the results of one plastic surgery opt for another procedure on a different body part. Tracey Karp is one of them. Happy with the results of her breast enlargement at age 17, she returned to her plastic surgeon two years later for a nose job.

"He did a breast augmentation on me two years ago," said Karp, who also lives in the Houston area. "And that went super well, so he made me feel very comfortable."

Teens' Favorites: Nose Jobs, Breast Enlargement

Karp was scheduled for surgery for a deviated septum when she asked her parents for permission to add rhinoplasty to the procedure. Knowing her yearning for the procedure, they agreed, in part to ensure that she was in the hands of a qualified surgeon.

"The fact that she was going to be shortly coming of age, where she could go out and do it behind our backs, we didn't want that to happen," her father, Jeff Karp, said.

Looks are a top concern for his daughter, who works out frequently at her gym. She calls herself "definitely obsessive" about her physical image.

"I put pressure on myself to look a certain way for sure, as, I would assume, most girls do at my age," Karp said. "I can always find things to change. I'm like, ugh, I'm only 19 and I have wrinkles."

Another favorite procedure among teen girls is breast augmentation, despite the Food and Drug Administration's having approved implants only for people 18 and older, although doctors are free to use their discretion for girls.

About 8,000 girls age 13 to 19 had their breasts enlarged last year, according to the American Society of Plastic Surgeons. And 2,953 of them were age 18 and younger.

EVALUATING THE AUTHOR'S ARGUMENTS:

Victoria Thompson's report features the stories of Caitlin Clemons and Tracey Karp. Write one to two paragraphs on each girl. Make sure to include why they decided to get plastic surgery, what procedure they had done, and how they felt afterwards. Then, state whether you approve of each girl's decision to get plastic surgery, and include how you formed your opinion.

Viewpoint

4

Plastic Surgery Can Result in Regret

Sabrina Weiss

"Despite everything [plastic] surgery did for me— and it did a lot—I wish I could undo it."

In the following viewpoint Sabrina Weiss shares the story of how she came to regret her nose job. She originally got plastic surgery because she had inherited her father's nose—a bumpy, imperfect nose that was neither slender nor feminine. For a while, plastic surgery made her feel more confident and might have helped attract people to her. But years later, as her father's death approached, she realized that by changing her nose, she had erased the physical bond she and her father once shared. She says that she regrets getting plastic surgery because it forever deleted the one physical feature she and her father shared. She concludes that as teens move beyond the phase of life in which they flirt and date, they will come to see their original body as an important and priceless piece of their history.

Weiss's comments on plastic surgery have appeared in *Elle* and on CNN.com.

1. How does Weiss describe her relationship with her father when she was about ten years old?
2. What does the author say represented her shortcomings as a girl?
3. What things has Weiss come to appreciate that she shares with her father?

Sailing up New York's Sprain Brook Parkway in my father's beige, ocean-liner-size Cadillac, I declared from the backseat: "I want a nose job." A few girls in my ninth-grade class had returned from winter vacation with snazzy new snouts, and I was resolved to do the same. I had, after all, inherited my father's nose, complete with its protruding bump and long, beakish tip. A cuter, daintier model, I argued, might soften my boyish face. Both of my parents wholeheartedly agreed. I wish I had a recording of the conversation so that I could replay the long sigh of relief that discharged from my mother's mouth.

A Father-Daughter Bond

My father married her later in life; by the time I was born, he was 50. Raised in a poor immigrant neighborhood in East New York, Brooklyn, he had cultivated a distinguished look and a self-styled British accent that gave him the enchanting air of Cary Grant. In all things, I sought his approval. At 10, I toiled alongside him in his workshop in our basement; later I took up his passions of writing and painting. He taught me to love [comedy team] Laurel & Hardy. Just as Hardy would lock eyes with the camera, expressing his irritation with Laurel's antics, my dad looked to me for understanding.

On a trip to California when I was 16, we left my mother and sister at the hotel; in the rental car, he told me we were on our way to an important meeting in Hollywood to discuss the possibility of producing his screenplay. It was a journey that could change his fate, and I was his chosen copilot.

Despite this bond, by the time I hit puberty, it was clear that, unlike my younger sister, Sophia—who was popular, well accessorized, and boy-crazy—I was not living up to his definition of womanhood. My

Plastic Surgery Is on the Decline Among Teens

The American Society for Aesthetic Plastic Surgery (ASAPS) reports that people younger than eighteen have received fewer plastic surgeries since 2001.

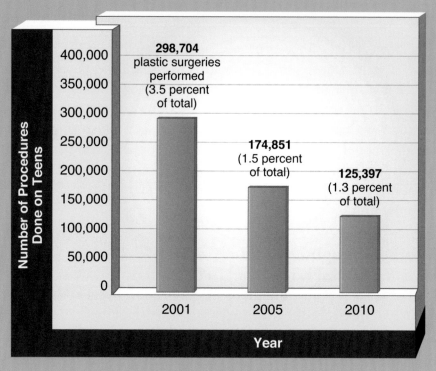

Taken from: American Society for Aesthetic Plastic Surgery (ASAPS), 2011.

father was born in 1928, the same year as Mickey Mouse, and possessed an old-fashioned, Disneyfied view of women: We should be soft, feminine, gentle—and constantly on a quest for our prince. Next to the label-conscious, salon-styled girls at my private school, I resembled a prepubescent boy, both aesthetically and spiritually. Rail thin, breasts hidden under oversize flannel shirts, I spent weekends wolfing down pizza and playing video games.

And then there was my nose—*his* nose—which grew more exaggerated at the onset of puberty. It became the focus of my self-loathing, a manifestation of all my shortcomings as a girl. Altering it was one way, at least, that I could become more feminine.

Did Plastic Surgery Make a Difference?

So, a few days after high school graduation, I finally got my nose job. The surgery flattened the bridge of my nose but left it with a lengthy tip and asymmetrical nostrils. A second procedure shaved down the tip and reshaped the nostrils. As promised, it made my face softer. Less self-conscious, I began to put more care into the way I dressed and even wore a little makeup.

But the anxious, tugging sensation in my chest was still there. Surgery eliminated the one problem that had so preoccupied me, but it forced me to acknowledge another, bigger issue—my sexuality—that would make me a failed woman in my father's eyes.

With time, I was able to crack my former self-perception. In college, I entered my first relationship with a woman and began to feel attractive and desirable—another first. I spent a semester in Florence, [Italy,] suspended in what seemed like a whirling dream of bicurious girls trying to bed me. Would that have been possible with my old nose?

> **FAST FACT**
>
> Dr. Tony Youn, a Michigan-based, board-certified plastic surgeon and contributor to MSNBC.com, estimates that up to 25 percent of patients who have nose jobs eventually undergo a corrective procedure because they complain they no longer look like themselves.

A Strained Relationship

I had spent my first postcollege year in San Francisco, but my father asked me to return to New York because of his waning health. Within a few weeks, I met a woman and one night accidentally fell asleep at her apartment, waking at 5 a.m. to discover 16 messages from my mother on my cell phone. I rushed home and tearfully came clean. My mother lambasted me for deceit and pronounced my sexuality a "phase."

From then on, my father was polite to me at family occasions, but increasingly distant. One Father's Day, I had a trophy made for him, which he received with indifference. When I bought tickets to

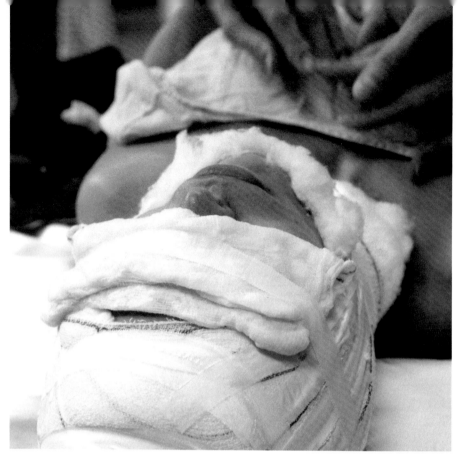

A woman recovers after plastic surgery. The author regretted her own surgery that changed her nose, a prominent family trait.

"Seeing Debussy, Hearing Monet" at Carnegie Hall for his birthday, he declined, blaming his health. My mother filled the gap, vilifying me and my "choices" even after I moved in with my girlfriend. She told me the news had aggravated my father's health, that he couldn't sleep at night because he was so distraught.

"I Wish I Could Undo It"

Until age 79, he spent his semiretired days in his Brooklyn law office, curled up with copies of *The New Yorker* and the *New York Post*, listening to a crackling radio and trading dirty jokes with the guys down the hall. But last November [2009], he was hospitalized after a fall, and it fell to me to pack up the office where he'd worked for more than 50 years. I uncovered unsold screenplays and short stories, illegible phone messages, and, at the very bottom of the pile, a stack of pictures. I flipped through them, snickering at the '70s sideburns and wide-collar shirts, until one gave me pause. It was my father's high school graduation portrait. Staring out from this glossy black-and-white photo was my own face: my closed-mouth smile; my dark, deep-set eyes. And there it was: my old nose. Despite everything the surgery did for me—and it did a lot—I wish I could undo it. At 31, I've come to appreciate the things I inherited from my father: his humor, his love of ketchup and Mondrian paintings. When he is gone, how will I reconcile my decision to erase something we once shared? I stared at the image, tears running down my cheeks.

I Erased Our Physical Bond

Soon afterward, my father entered hospice care. Twice, his lungs filled with fluid, and he narrowly escaped death. But while his body hangs on precariously, his mind remains remarkably intact. I've spent more time with him this year than over the previous 10, our relationship reduced to its purest form: a father and daughter who have a lot in common and care for one another. We talk or watch Laurel & Hardy while he keeps the nurses laughing with puns and one-liners. It's both a gift and some kind of cosmic joke.

In the end, this is what we're left with: an aging parent wasting away in a hospital room, muscle and fat disappearing from his body. When I visit him each week, I scan his face: eyes, cheeks, mouth, chin. My gaze stops at the nose, and I bring my right hand to my face and run my index finger along the bridge of my own.

> ## EVALUATING THE AUTHOR'S ARGUMENTS:
>
> Even though plastic surgery made Sabrina Weiss more confident and attractive, she lost a meaningful and irreplaceable connection to her father. She did not foresee this consequence when she had the procedure as a young girl. What other unforeseen consequences might plastic surgery carry? In a short essay of one to two paragraphs, come up with at least two. Then, state whether you think these consequences outweigh the perceived benefits of plastic surgery.

Avoiding Media Can Improve Body Image

Amanda Leigh Brozana

"Until advertisers offer us a more realistic view of the world, it's important to take steps to improve our own perception of our bodies, and that may require tuning out."

Tuning out media and advertisements helps people improve their body image, argues Amanda Leigh Brozana in the following viewpoint. She argues that advertisements, photos, and other media torment people with unrealistic images of bodies that are impossible for most to attain. Rather than feeling horrible, she thinks it is better to avoid media. She knows this works, because during one point in her life when she exposed herself mainly only to the news, she felt more self-confident than she ever had—despite weighing more than she ever had. When she decided to lose weight, she did so because she wanted to be more physically capable, not because she wanted to look like models in magazines. Brozana concludes that advertisers are unlikely to stop tormenting people with unrealistic images, but people can feel better if they simply tune them out.

Brozana is a regular contributor to the *Washington Times*, a daily District of Columbia newspaper.

AS YOU READ, CONSIDER THE FOLLOWING QUESTIONS:
1. What does Brozana say she is supposed to feel ashamed about?
2. How much did the author weigh during the years she felt most self-confident?
3. What, according to Brozana, is as important for parents to discuss with their children as sex?

Today, I'm breaking one of the sacred rules for women. I am 164 lbs. and 5'6". I know, I know. Women are never supposed to reveal their weight. If we do, we're clearly not supposed to tell the truth unless that number is well within the bounds of making a doctor suspicious of an eating disorder.

Women Become Paralyzed

In 2011 at 164 lbs., I'm supposed to feel ashamed, uncomfortable, hide from cameras while searching for the next greatest diet. And some days, for the most part, that's just what I do. A poor body image that often paralyzes women has been linked to advertising for years and has even made us reconsider the real beauty of unquestionable icons like Marilyn Monroe and Jane Russell.

Why is body image so important to women? Studies tell us that if women are more confident, even if they are not very attractive by advertisers' standards, they are more likely to find happiness in social situations, relationships, jobs, and their overall lives.

Advertisers Torment Us

However, it's not just the preoccupation with weight that contributes to low body image. Advertisers are more than happy to point out what is wrong with the American woman: wrinkles and lines; gray, dull or out of place hair; pimples, freckles, blotchy or dry skin; darkness or bags under the eyes; short, light-colored lashes or overly bushy brows; arm and thigh flab. The list of things that makes one less-than-beautiful goes on and on.

In [2011] Britain's Advertising Standards Authority [ASA] made headlines by banning two ads, including [actress] Julia Roberts and [model] Christy Turlington because the women were "too photoshopped," something the ASA thought would be very misleading for consumers of L'Oreal beauty products. In addition, ASA took a stand against *Vogue* magazine's use of a 10-year-old model lying seductively on a bed, showing prepubescent near-cleavage in a dress cut to the navel and her face seductively made up.

Legislation Can Only Do So Much

I'll leave for another time just how much of true childhood remains for children in the 21st century, though clearly anyone who sees even one image from the 15-page *Vogue* spread of little Thylane Blondeau would know the answer.

Yet even as ASA is starting to take action to protect media consumers from images that push the boundaries of reality for perfect bodies from feet to face, British women revealed in a recent poll that they have a poorer body image than do their U.S. counterparts.

I think Britain's ASA may have the right idea. Cracking down on companies that produce images of unrealistic body expectations has spurred debate about what defines beauty and what is acceptable. However, I'd argue that if we really want to make a more realistic and lasting change in our perception of ourselves, tuning out might be a better solution.

Avoiding Media Can Help

For several years I rarely watched TV, except for news. The few magazines and many websites I visited were news-related and I, thankfully, lived in an area where there were few billboards and fewer shops that displayed 30-foot posters of slender models.

For those few years, as I grew from about 155 to 180 lbs., I felt better about myself than I ever have when fully immersed in the

Tuning out all media and beauty advertisements helps people improve their body image, the author argues.

entertainment-oriented media. My body image was based on a comparison with those around me.

Since more than one-third of all U.S. adults are overweight and another third are obese, according to the Centers for Disease Control [and Prevention], I fit right in. Don't get me wrong, we should all make our health a priority, but often what is a healthy body weight is not one that would make us eligible to grace the pages of fashion magazines.

Listen to Your Body

When I did consider the need to lose weight, it was based on the fact that I was feeling more winded when taking the stairs or I had noticed pain in my lower back and my feet. My desire to lose weight wasn't based on social expectations but on my body's feedback. The pressure internally to become healthier was a better motivator than

What Promotes Positive Body Image?

In 2009 *Glamour* magazine polled sixteen thousand women on what made them feel good or bad about their bodies.

"Which of the following makes you feel good about yourself/ have a positive image of your body?"

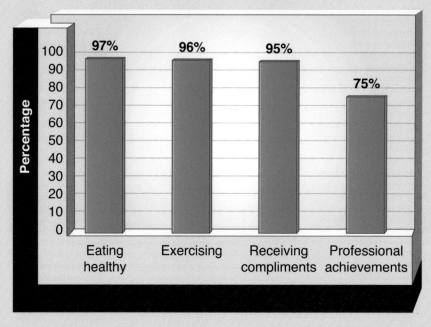

Taken from: Shaun Dreisback. "16,000 Women Tell Their Body Confidence Secrets." *Glamour*, March 23, 2009.

any external factor like trying to slim down to attract men or fit into this year's cutest bikini.

Clearly, unplugging even slightly is a difficult task since so much of our world revolves around media. Teens, especially, are so plugged in that to ask them to ignore the media entirely would be impossible. However, looking around their own social network to find realistic body images rather than relying on the media's messages might be a good start.

Until advertisers offer us a more realistic view of the world, it's important to take steps to improve our own perception of our bodies, and that may require tuning out those images and tuning into the world around us.

Tune Out Images That Sabotage You

I'm not a parent, so I try to refrain from saying what parents should do with their children. However, I believe all parents want their children to grow up with healthy self-esteem. Talking to children about body image can be as important as talking to them about sex. What's more important, though, may be the choices parents make for their children at a young age regarding clothing and media consumption. Parents who buy their young daughters clothes that sexualize them are not only buying into advertising hype, but they are also sending the message that their value is based on the ability to make others lust after them.

Moving away from the skewed messages of advertisers and the media of what's right and wrong and what's age appropriate, messages that clearly don't meet real world standards, may be hard, but it may also be the best thing we do for ourselves and the next generation.

EVALUATING THE AUTHOR'S ARGUMENTS:

Amanda Leigh Brozana admits that tuning out all media is impossible to do in the twenty-first century—especially for teens. Still, she says, people can make choices about what media to avoid. Consider the kinds of images and messages you are exposed to each day. Are there ones that make you feel bad about yourself? If so, which ones? Conduct an experiment in which you avoid those images and messages for three days in a row. Do you feel more confident than normal? Write a three-paragraph essay on your experience.

Facts About Body Image

Editor's note: These facts can be used in reports or papers to reinforce or add credibility when making important points or claims.

Facts About Body Image and Self-Esteem

A 2008 survey conducted by the Dove Campaign for Real Beauty found the following about self-esteem and body image:

- 70 percent of girls believe they are not "good enough."
- 70 percent of girls feel they are inadequate in at least one area, including their looks, performance in school, and/or their relationships with friends and family members.
- 62 percent of girls feel insecure or unsure of themselves.
- 57 percent of girls have a mother who criticizes her own looks.
- 75 percent of girls with low self-esteem reported engaging in negative activities such as disordered eating, cutting, bullying, smoking, or drinking when they feel bad about themselves (compared with 25 percent of girls with high self-esteem).
- 61 percent of girls with low self-esteem admit to talking badly about themselves (compared with 15 percent of girls with high self-esteem).
- 25 percent of girls with low self-esteem resort to hurting themselves on purpose when they feel bad about themselves (compared with 4 percent of girls with high self-esteem).
- 25 percent of girls with low self-esteem report either starving themselves, refusing to eat, or overeating and throwing up when they feel bad about themselves (compared with 7 percent of girls with high self-esteem).
- 67 percent of girls aged 13 to 17 turn to their mother as a resource when they feel bad about themselves (compared with 91 percent of girls aged 8 to 12).
- Just 27 percent of girls aged 13 to 17 turn to their father for help when they feel bad about themselves (compared with 54 percent of girls aged 8 to 12).

- More than one-third (34 percent) of girls with low self-esteem believe that they are not a good enough daughter (compared with 9 percent of girls with high self-esteem).
- 93 percent of girls with low self-esteem want their parents to change their behavior toward them in at least one way (compared with 73 percent for girls with high self-esteem).

A 2009 survey of more than a thousand women, conducted by the Dove Campaign for Real Beauty, found:
- 96 percent said models featured in beauty advertisements do not realistically represent women.
- 40 percent said such ads made them self-conscious about their appearance.
- More than 25 percent said they feel inadequate after viewing such ads.
- 20 percent said such images make them less confident in their daily lives.
- 95 percent of those polled said they want to see more realistic photos of women used in beauty advertising.
- 58 percent thought they could tell the difference between images that had been airbrushed and those that had not.
- 42 percent said they could not tell the difference.
- 96 percent said advertisers should be honest about the extent to which they digitally alter photos.

A 2011 poll taken by *Girl's Life* magazine found the following about readers' body image and self-esteem:
- 80 percent of readers find fault with their bodies.
- More than 50 percent of readers said they have skipped meals or thrown up to lose weight.
- 81 percent of readers said they had a favorite body part.
- 54 percent of readers said they appreciate that their bodies help them do fun things.
- 80 percent of readers had dieted to lose weight.
- 64 percent of readers said seeing pictures of ultra-skinny models and celebrities discourages them.
- 40 percent of readers named Taylor Swift as the ideal body type.
- 47 percent of readers said they feel better about their bodies when they tell themselves they look great.

- 78 percent of readers say when asked by a friend whether the friend looks fat, they always say "no."
- 39 percent of readers say their weight makes them feel bad.

Facts About Teens and Plastic Surgery

According to the American Society for Aesthetic Plastic Surgery (ASAPS):

- In 2010 there was a decrease in the overall number of cosmetic surgeries on teenagers (those eighteen and younger).
- Ear surgery was the most popular surgical procedure in 2010 for teens.
- Rhinoplasty (nose job) was the most requested aesthetic surgical procedure by teens.
- Laser hair removal and chemical peels were the most popular nonsurgical procedures performed on teens in 2010.
- In 2001 there were 298,704 procedures performed on those 18 and younger, representing 3.5 percent of the total surgeries performed that year.
- In 2005 there were 174,851 procedures performed on those 18 and younger, representing 1.5 percent of the total surgeries performed that year.
- In 2009 there were 203,308 procedures performed on those 18 and younger, representing 2.0 percent of the total surgeries performed that year.
- In 2010 there were 125,397 procedures performed on those 18 and younger, representing 1.3 percent of the total surgeries performed that year.
- In 2010 there were 1,798 lipoplasty procedures performed on those 18 and younger.
- In 2010 there were 4,153 breast augmentation procedures performed on girls 18 and under, representing 1.3 percent of the total number of breast augmentation procedures. The reasons for these breast augmentations were largely medical.

Facts About Eating Disorders

According to the National Association of Anorexia Nervosa and Associated Disorders:

- Up to 24 million people of all ages and both genders suffer from an eating disorder (anorexia, bulimia, and binge-eating disorder) in the United States.
- An estimated 0.5 to 3.7 percent of women suffer from anorexia nervosa in their lifetime.
- About 1 percent of female adolescents have anorexia.
- An estimated 1.1 to 4.2 percent of women have bulimia nervosa in their lifetime.
- An estimated 2 to 5 percent of Americans experience binge-eating disorder in a six-month period.
- An estimated 10 to 15 percent of people with anorexia or bulimia are male.
- Only one in ten men and women with eating disorders receive treatment. Men are less likely to seek treatment for eating disorders because of the perception that they are "women's diseases."
- Among gay men, nearly 14 percent appear to suffer from bulimia and over 20 percent appear to be anorexic.
- About half of all people who have suffered from anorexia develop bulimia or bulimic habits.
- Almost 50 percent of people with eating disorders meet the criteria for depression.
- Only 35 percent of people that receive treatment for eating disorders get treatment at a specialized facility for eating disorders.
- Eating disorders have the highest mortality rate of any mental illness.
- The mortality rate associated with anorexia nervosa is twelve times higher than the death rate associated with all causes of death for females fifteen to twenty-four years old.
- 20 percent of people suffering from anorexia will prematurely die from complications related to their eating disorder, including suicide and heart problems.

A 2009 study published in the *American Journal of Psychiatry* looked at the high mortality rates associated with eating disorders, including the following data:
- 4 percent of anorexia nervosa sufferers die.
- Nearly 4 percent (3.9 percent) of bulimia nervosa sufferers die.
- Over 5 percent (5.2 percent) of people who suffer from a non-specified eating disorder die.

Organizations to Contact

The editors have compiled the following list of organizations concerned with the issues debated in this book. The descriptions are derived from materials provided by the organizations. All have publications or information available for interested readers. The list was compiled on the date of publication of the present volume; the information provided here may change. Be aware that many organizations take several weeks or longer to respond to inquiries, so allow as much time as possible for the receipt of requested materials.

Academy for Eating Disorders (AED)
111 Deer Lake Rd., Ste. 100
Deerfield, IL 60015
(847) 498-4274
website: www.aedweb.org

The AED is a global, multidisciplinary professional organization that provides cutting-edge professional training and education; inspires new developments in eating disorders research, prevention, and clinical treatments; and is the international source for state-of-the-art information in the field of eating disorders.

Advocates for Youth
2000 M St. NW, Ste. 750
Washington, DC 20036
(202) 419-3420
website: www.advocatesforyouth.org

Established in 1980 as the Center for Population Options, Advocates for Youth champions efforts that help young people make informed and responsible decisions about their reproductive and sexual health. Pamphlets, articles, and outreach services address a variety of issues that intersect with body image.

Alliance for Eating Disorders Awareness
PO Box 2562
West Palm Beach, FL 33402
(866) 662-1235
e-mail: info@eatingdisorderinfo.org
website: www.allianceforeatingdisorders.com

This organization seeks to establish easily accessible programs across the nation that allow children and young adults the opportunity to learn about eating disorders and the positive effects of a healthy body image. Its aim is to disseminate educational information to parents and caregivers about the warning signs, dangers, and consequences of anorexia, bulimia, and other related disorders.

American Psychiatric Association
1000 Wilson Blvd., Ste. 1825
Arlington, VA 22209-3901
(703) 907-7300
e-mail: apa@psych.org
website: www.psych.org

The American Psychiatric Association is an organization of psychiatrists dedicated to studying the nature, treatment, and prevention of mental disorders, including those that contribute to eating disorders. It helps create mental health policies, distributes information about psychiatry, and promotes psychiatric research and education.

American Psychological Association (APA)
750 First St. NE, Washington, DC 20002-4242
(202) 336-5500 • toll-free: (800) 374-2721
e-mail: public.affairs@apa.org
website: www.apa.org

A scientific and professional organization that represents psychologists in the United States, the APA is the largest association of psychologists worldwide, with 150,000 members. It produces numerous publications on eating disorders and other topics related to psychology.

The Center for the Study of Anorexia and Bulimia (CASB)
1841 Broadway, 4th Fl.
New York, NY 10023

(212) 333-3444
e-mail: csab@icpnyc.org
website: http://csabnyc.org

The CASB is the oldest nonprofit eating disorders clinic in New York City. It is devoted to treating individuals with eating disorders and training the professionals who work with them.

Children's Body-Image Foundation
1151 W. Fifth Ave.
Columbus, OH 43212
(614) 288-9155
website: http://childrensbodyimagefoundation.org

The Children's Body-Image Foundation believes that all children should feel good about themselves. The foundation strives to help children build self-esteem, self-confidence, and self-acceptance by raising body-image awareness and helping to educate the public.

Eating Disorders Coalition for Research, Policy, and Action
720 Seventh St. NW, Ste. 300
Washington, DC 20001
(202) 543-9570
e-mail: manager@eatingdisorderscoalition.org
website: www.eatingdisorderscoalition.org

The mission of the Eating Disorders Coalition for Research, Policy, and Action is to advance the federal recognition of eating disorders as a public health priority.

National Association of Anorexia Nervosa and
Associated Disorders (ANAD)
PO Box 640
Naperville, IL 60566
helpline: (630) 577-1330
website: www.anad.org

ANAD offers hotline counseling, operates an international network of support groups for people with eating disorders and their families, and provides referrals to health care professionals who treat eating disorders. It produces a quarterly newsletter and information packets and organizes national conferences and local programs. All ANAD services are provided free of charge.

National Eating Disorders Association (NEDA)
155 W. Forty-Sixth St.
New York, NY 10036
e-mail: info@nationaleatingdisorders.org
website: www.nationaleatingdisorders.org

NEDA is dedicated to promoting the awareness and prevention of eating disorders by encouraging positive self-esteem and size acceptance. It provides free and low-cost educational information on eating disorders and their prevention.

Society for Adolescent Medicine (SAM)
1916 NW Copper Oaks Cir., Blue Springs, MO 64015
(816) 224-8010
website: www.adolescenthealth.org

SAM is a multidisciplinary organization of professionals committed to improving the physical and psychosocial health and well-being of all adolescents. It helps plan and coordinate national and international professional education programs on adolescent health. Its publications include the monthly *Journal of Adolescent Health* and the quarterly *SAM Newsletter*.

For Further Reading

Books

Adatto, Kiku. *Picture Perfect: Life in the Age of the Photo Op.* Princeton, NJ: Princeton University Press, 2008. Examines the use and abuse of images today, and how evolving technologies make it easier than ever to capture, manipulate, and spread images.

Bailey, Eric J. *Black America, Body Beautiful: How the African American Image Is Changing Fashion, Fitness, and Other Industries.* Santa Barbara, CA: Praeger, 2008. Spotlights African American views on body image and explores how these views are influencing fashion, advertising, fitness, and other areas.

Brittingham, Kimberly. *Read My Hips: How I Learned to Love My Body, Ditch Dieting, and Live Large.* New York: Three Rivers, 2011. This writer and blogger offers a memoir about her lifelong relationships with food, dieting, and body image.

Redd, Nancy Amanda. *Body Drama: Real Girls, Real Bodies, Real Issues, Real Answers.* New York: Gotham, 2007. Written by a former Miss America swimsuit competition winner, this book approaches body image with humor and medical accuracy.

Periodicals and Internet Sources

Alexander, Hilary. "Keep 'Skinny Model' Debate in Perspective," *Daily Telegraph (London),* January 26, 2007. http://fashion.tele graph.co.uk/columns/hilary-alexander/TMG3358471/Keep -skinny-model-debate-in-perspective.html.

Bloom, Amy. "Dear Every Woman I Know, Including Me," *O, the Oprah Magazine,* November 2011. www.oprah.com/spirit /Improving-Body-Image-How-to-Feel-Beautiful-Improving-Self -Esteem.

Brooks, Karen. "Fed Up with Faking It," *Courier Mail* (Brisbane, Australia), February 24, 2010. www.couriermail.com.au/spike /columnists/fed-up-with-faking-it/story-e6frerfo-1225833572711.

Davis, Erin. "Don't Blame Barbie," LiesYoungWomenBelieve.com, July 8, 2009. www.liesyoungwomenbelieve.com/index.php?id=293.

Diller, Vivian. "Is Photoshop Destroying America's Body Image?," *HuffingtonPost*, July 7, 2011. www.huffingtonpost.com/vivian -diller-phd/photoshop-body-image_b_891095.html.

Dillingham, Maud. "Life-Size Barbie: What's the Big Deal?," *Christian Science Monitor,* April 20, 2011. www.csmonitor.com /The-Culture/2011/0420/Life-size-Barbie-What-s-the-big-deal.

Dragone, Davide, and Luca Savorelli. "Thinness and Obesity: A Model of Food Consumption, Health Concerns, and Social Pressure," Economic Organisation and Public Policy Programme, The Suntory and Toyota International Centres for Economics and Related Disciplines, EOPP 2010/17. http://sticerd.lse.ac.uk/dps /eopp/eopp17.pdf.

Gold, Tanya. "L'Oreal's Pulled Adverts: This Ideal of Female Beauty Is an Abomination," *Guardian* (Manchester, UK), July 29, 2011. www.guardian.co.uk/commentisfree/2011/jul/29/loreal-adverts -pulled-by-asa-beauty-tanya-gold.

Kaplan, Karen. "'Maggie Goes on a Diet' the Sensible Way in Children's Book," *Los Angeles Times,* August 23, 2011. http://articles .latimes.com/2011/aug723/news/la-heb-maggie-goes-on-a-diet -book-20110823.

Leong, Irene. "Obsession of the Size Zero Kind," *Sun Daily* (Malaysia), September 23, 2011. www.thesundaily.my/news/154545.

Lohr, Steve. "Software to Rate How Drastically Photos Are Retouched," *New York Times,* November 29, 2011. www.nytimes .com/2011/11/29/technology/software-to-rate-how-drastically -photos-are-retouched.html.

Lyster-Mensh, Laura Collins. "Why *Maggie's Diet* Is a Bad Idea," *HuffingtonPost*, September 7, 2011. www.huffingtonpost.com /laura-collins-lystermensh/why-maggies-diet-is-a-bad_b_949050 .html.

Marcus, Bonnie. "Does This Article Make Me Look Fat?," *Forbes,* September 29, 2011. www.forbes.com/sites/bonniemarcus /2011/09/29/does-this-article-make-me-look-fat/.

Martin, Michael. "Asian-Americans and the Quest for Thin," National Public Radio.com, January 3, 2011. www.npr.org /2011/01/03/132628275/Asian-Americans-And-The-Quest-For -Thin.

McPherson, Katherine. "Barbie Can Teach Girls About More than Body Image," *Oklahoma Daily* (University of Oklahoma), October 17, 2011. http://oudaily.com/news/2011/oct/17/column-barbie-can-teach-girls-about-more-body-imag/.

Murphy, Sarah. "Wiggle and Jiggle: Why the Media Needs to Change," *Mount Holyoke (MA) News,* October 20, 2011. http://themh news.org/2011/10/op-ed/wiggle-and-jiggle-why-the-media-needs-to-change.

Penny, Laurie. "Child Anorexia: Is 'Size-Zero Culture' Really to Blame?," *Guardian* (Manchester, UK), August 2, 2011. http://www.guardian.co.uk/commentisfree/2011/aug/02/child-anorexia-size-zero.

Razer, Helen. "At Least Women in Burqas Are Not Judged on Their Looks," *Sydney Morning Herald,* September 18, 2009. http://www.smh.com.au/opinion/at-least-women-in-burqas-are-not-judged-on-their-looks-20090918-fuwc.html.

Resnikoff, Ned. "H&M Whittles Down Acceptable Body Types to Exactly One," *Ms. Magazine,* December 6, 2011. http://msmaga zine.com/blog/blog/2011/12/06/hm-whittles-acceptable-body-types-down-to-exactly-one/.

Rodriguez, Lavinia. "Who Are We Trying to Please with Body Image?," *St. Petersburg (FL) Times,* July 2, 2011.

Rubenstein, Grace. "Boys and Body Image: Eating Disorders Don't Discriminate," Edutopia, February 18, 2010. www.edutopia.org/boys-eating-disorders.

Squires, Dara. "In Water We Are All Weightless—of Mermaids and Whales," *Western Star* (Alberta, Canada), October 19, 2010. www.thewesternstar.com/Opinion/Columns/2011-10-19/article-2780606/In-water-we-are-all-weightless-%26mdash%3B-of-mermaids-and-whales/1.

Toub, Micah. "It's the Worry, Not the Weight," *Globe & Mail* (Toronto), October 14, 2011.

Tuohy, Wendy. "Banning Airbrushed Ads Proves We Have Belatedly Come of Age," *Herald Sun* (Melbourne, Australia), August 3, 2011. www.heraldsun.com.au/opinion/banning-airbrushed-ads-proves-we-have-belatedly-come-of-age/story-e6frfhqf-1226106940337.

Von Furstenberg, Diane, and David Herzog. "Healthier Standards," The Council of Fashion Designers in America, March 8, 2011. www.cfda.com/healthier-standards-an-op-ed-by-cfda-president -diane-von-furstenberg-and-director-of-the-harris-center-dr-david -herzog/.

Woods, Theresa L. "America's Broken Body Image," Back\slash, February 6, 2011. http://backslashonline.com/index.php ?option=com_k2&view=item&id=674:americas-broken-body -image&Itemid=41.

Websites

Adios Barbie (www.adiosbarbie.com).This site encourages girls and women to say *adios* (good-bye) to a negative body image and hello to a positive self-image. It accomplishes this through a wide variety of articles, blog posts, videos, and other multimedia.

Anorexia Nervosa and Related Eating Disorders, Inc. (www.anred .com). This nonprofit group is an authoritative source for informa-tion about anorexia nervosa, bulimia nervosa, binge-eating disorder, compulsive exercising, and other lesser-known food and weight disorders, including details about recovery and prevention.

BodiMojo (www.bodimojo.com). This site, sponsored by Northeastern University, features interactive games, diaries, chat forums, and other tools that seek to improve teens' body image.

My Body Gallery (www.mybodygallery.com). This website encour-ages women to post anonymous, discreet photos of their bodies to promote accurate body image. Photos are searchable by height, weight, and clothing size. The editors hope to create a compre-hensive database that helps women more objectively see what they look like.

National Organization for Women's Love Your Body Campaign (http://loveyourbody.nowfoundation.org). This site, run by the National Organization for Women (NOW), seeks to wipe out narrow beauty standards, superficial gender stereotypes, and the portrayal of women as a sexual commodity.

Operation Beautiful (http://operationbeautiful.com). This website seeks to reduce negative self-talk, also known as "fat talk." It encourages people to leave positive messages, such as "You are beautiful!" in random public places to counteract negativity from advertisements.

Our Bodies, Ourselves (www.ourbodiesourselves.org). This is the website companion to the classic book *Our Bodies, Ourselves,* which promotes positive body image and women's health.

Something Fishy (www.something-fishy.org). This website contains a wealth of information on a variety of eating disorders. Through articles, blog posts, and first-person testimonials, it seeks to promote positive body image among women and men of all ages and races.

Index

Breast augmentation surgery, 91, 93

British Fashion Council (BFC), 54, 83–84, 85, 86, 87

British Journal of Health Psychology, 8

Brozana, Amanda Leigh, 100

Cable, Paul, 50

Campaign for a Commercial-Free Childhood, 26

Campaign for Body Confidence (UK), 39

Campbell, Naomi, 81

Celebrities, often airbrushed, *56*

Centers for Disease Control and Prevention, 103

Clemons, Caitlin, 91

Cochrane, Kira, 77

Colbert, Stephen, 70

Cole, Lily, 83

Cook, Rachael Leigh, 43, *44, 45*

Copeland, Libby, 69

Cortez, Marjorie, 64

Crawford, Cindy, 81

Dangin, Pascal, 52, 53–54, 57

Davis, Geena, 43

Deeley, Cat, 55

Devices and Desires (Tone), 73

Digital enhancement
    of advertisements is positive, 42–45
    girls' awareness of, 8–9
    public is aware of/accepts, 51–57

Ditto, Beth, 78

Dove Campaign for Real Beauty, 8, 16, 52, 78

Dove Ultimate Go Sleeveless campaign, 70, 72, 75

Dragone, Davide, 86

Dydek, Margo, 66

Eating disorders/related behaviors, 14
    among black *vs.* white women, *31*
    among men, 23–24
    among youth, 32
    fashion industry is not responsible for, 87–88
    increase among African-American women, 32
    men as percentage of total sufferers of, *27*

Ephron, Nora, 75

Esquire (magazine), 75

Evangelista, Linda, 81

Fashion industry
    emphasis on thin models by, 77–81
    is not to blame for poor body image, 82–89

Featherstone, Lynne, 39

Fox, Stephen, 71

Girl Scout Research Institute, 49

Girls/women
    ad campaigns directed at, 70–71
    body image problems are cross-cultural among, 29–34

Picture Credits

© Antiques & Collectables/Alamy, 13

© AP Images/Junji Kurokawa, 103

© Scott Camazine/Photo Researchers, Inc., 35

© Corbis Flirt/Alamy, 25

© Dan Pearson Photography/Alamy, 10

© Simon Dawson/Bloomberg via Getty Images, 72

© Benedicte Desrus/Alamy, 76

© Ian Francis/Alamy, 47

Gale/Cengage Learning, 15, 27, 31, 49, 56, 60, 67, 74, 80, 96, 104

© David J. Green--Lifestyle themes/Alamy, 20

© Nick Harvey/Wire Image/Getty Images, 84

© Yvonne Hemsey/Getty Images, 92

© MJ Kim/Getty Images, 40

© Paul Morigi/WireImage/Getty Images, 44

© Leon Neal/AFP/Getty Images, 79

© Oleksiy Maksymenko Photography/Alamy, 33

© Phanie/Photo Researchers, Inc., 98

© Patrick Riviere/Getty Images

© Oli Scarff/Getty Images, 55

© Arthur Turner/Alamy, 62

© WoodyStock/Alamy, 65